CONNECTING
HEART
WITH
HEAD

The Easy Way to Make EVERYDAY
life magical by opening the pineal
gland of the brain

MUSHTAQ H. JAAFRI

authorHOUSE®

AuthorHouse™
1663 Liberty Drive
Bloomington, IN 47403
www.authorhouse.com
Phone: 1 (800) 839-8640

Published by AuthorHouse 09/27/2017

ISBN: 978-1-5462-0953-9 (sc)
ISBN: 978-1-5462-0952-2 (e)

Print information available on the last page.

Any people depicted in stock imagery provided by Thinkstock are models, and such images are being used for illustrative purposes only. Certain stock imagery © Thinkstock.

This book is printed on acid-free paper.

CONTENTS

Award-Winning
Author of
Go With the Flow! . . .

Mushtaq H. Jaafri

"We can remain at peace. We can
never control God, but we can
Align and flow with his will."

John-Roger—*Spiritual Warrior Book!*

DISCLAIMER

In writing about spiritual concepts, I have inevitably used words that mean different things to different people, depending upon either the personal path they have taken or their spiritual or religious upbringing. In the pages that follow, I've words like "Soul," "soul," "Spirit," "spirit," "Self," "self," "God," and others in specific ways. To get the most out of this book, I suggest readers suspend, as much as possible, their personal interpretations of these words and concepts and stay open to how I define them in context, by my explanations, and by their own intuitive sense. There have been very few teachings that declare that the man is to gain his identity through the right side and into God. Inside of us who we are as an eternal being meets the person who is the there temporarily. Here the Spirit, the emanation from God, meets us, the self we know. This is our point of convergence. The joy of alignment flows over into everything you do, including the most mundane aspects of your day-to-day life.

ACKNOWLEDGMENT

It takes a collaborated effort of many professional people to produce a worthwhile self-help or personal development book. My special thanks go to Dr. Paul Kaye D.S.S, for taking the John-Roger, *the founder of MSIA,* lecture notes, and skillfully recognizing the book, that inspired the major motion picture *"Spiritual Warrior."* To Laren Bright for reviewing my original manuscript, *Connecting Heart With Head,* and saw the vision of the **message through my eyes.** To **Buddy Dow**, my agent at the **Author House** for supporting me through the production process. My special thanks **go to Debbie Roth, MSIA – Soul Awareness Seminars Coordinator,** who has *already* seen the vision of MSIA as a world teaching—truly a world teaching. Finally, my thanks go to **John Morton D.S.S, - MSIA Spiritual Director** who is one of my heroes and role models for the *Spiritual Warrior.* who I meet at the Rukmini-Canal in the Realms of Spirit during my nightly spiritual exercises.

Thank You.

DEDICATION

This book is dedicated to John-Roger, the founder of the *Movement of the Spiritual Inner Awareness,* (MSIA). This book is based on J-R's New York Times' best seller book that inspired the major motion picture the *Spiritual Warrior.* **John-Roger** intuitively saw this book in it because it takes you from where the original book left you. This book is a living proof of what J-R taught: *The mantle of the Spiritual Warrior is attainable by everyone."* For thirty-five years, the author has truly lived the Spiritual Warrior type life-style on a daily basis. It has assisted him in converging his spirit back into alignment—*literally!*

How to Work this Book?

A Road Map to Soul Awareness

If you look at a road map of how to get from New York to Los Angeles, California, you'll see just a series of markings on a piece of paper, Los Angeles is unknown to you.

You can sit and look at this map forever, but it will never physically take you there. But once you get in your car and drive, the map becomes a reference point of what really exists.

And seeing what is really there lets you know the accuracy or inaccuracy of the information on the map. After you have been over the territory and experienced it for yourself, you see how it fits together.

Then you can trust the map enough to give it someone else and say, *"This can get your there."* I have truly followed the map for thirty-five years to its outermost edges, and experiencing all for myself and I can say to you that *trust* what has been written here with a kind of faith in it, a kind of hope in it, a kind of belief in it until you do it and it works for you. This book will become a road map for you to get from where you are now—***spiritually,*** to where you want to be.

Just get in your car and drive (so to speak) this book will become a reference point of what really exists and seeing what is really there will let you know the accuracy of the information. ***Align yourself by training your attention on your intention; the convergence will shift in its own time to know God.***

FOREWORD

Dr. Mushtaq Jaafri has been searching for spiritual truth his whole life. In this, his latest book, he puts all his knowledge together and offers readers a path to true happiness which does not involve the accumulation of wealth and material things, but does involve being kind, helping others, acting honorably and just being the kind of person that would be called a true friend. Dr. Jaafri shows us how to be an observer of our thoughts, a way to silence our incessant mind and overcome feelings of anger, hatred, doubt and worry. It is an ongoing process but one that is achievable even in this day and age. He gives you a glimpse into his own life, his shortcomings and how he overcame them and provides you with the simple tools to make your life easier each and every day. You will discover that we are spiritual beings in human bodies and how to connect to that spirit whenever you want to. You will learn what happens in near-death experiences and you will be able to overcome your fears to seek the life you truly deserve. Get ready for the journey of your lifetime. Enjoy this book. Share it with friends. May true peace follow you in all of life's endeavors.

Al Galasso, Executive Director, National Association of Book Entrepreneurs. (NABE).

The Plan of This Book

Excerpt from the book: *Spiritual Warrior* – by John-Roger, D.S.S

"When we incorporate these characteristics into everything we do, they steer us toward our intention. But the task of developing these characteristics and becoming a Spiritual Warrior is formidable. As you begin your training in Spiritual Warriorhood, remember that its purpose is to affirm and strengthen the best inside of you and to support you in reaping the abundance that this world has to offer."

More importantly, we need to practice being in Spirit, being in alignment with our spiritual intention, so that it becomes our habitual state. This book will not waste your time by attempting to change your behavior or rid you of your negative patterns. Such attempts are invariably futile. You won't find any easy way to lose weight, quit smoking, or make a million dollars in these pages.

However, changes will take place naturally as you adopt the simple principles and tools offered in the *Fifteen*

Spiritual Exercises in this book that represents a kind of advanced training that will allow you to put into practice the principles you have learned. My spiritual teacher said to me: ***"The mantle of the Spiritual Warrior is attainable by everyone, but it requires a different way of proceeding through life, one which will challenge you.***

"I'll say 'amen' to that because for thirty-five years, I did take this challenge. But, you know what? Those of us who do practice the art of the Spiritual Warrior will find that the rewards are tremendous. *It is the satisfaction that come to all who conquer self and force life to pay whatever is asked.* **I've found what I was looking for in my search for meaning of life and paid every price for it.**

CRITICAL CLAIM

FOR THE BOOK

"This is a beautiful book of Mushtaq Jaafri's journey into greater Soul awareness. He shares keys that helped him along the way, including how he came to be of service as a Soul Awareness Seminar Leader through the Movement of Spiritual Inner Awareness.

Each one of his chapters is laid out with compassion, caring, and earnestness to share about the Spirit. Thanks for the opportunity to read how one man's experience can touch us all." **Debbie Roth, D.S.S. – MSIA Minister**

I believe all of us are on a journey of greater learning and awareness in our lives. Mushtaq shares his spiritual experiences in a relatable way with joyful enthusiasm.

There are lots of passages of value to be found in this book which can assist one to discover the Divinity within.- **Mark Lurie, MSIA minister**

Connecting Heart with Head offers a compelling explanation of humanity's relationship to the divine and guidance on how to develop and nurture our understanding of and integration of the spiritual into our lives. Your passion for the subject and the inclusion of stories from your own experience enliven the narrative and help make your information concrete for readers.

Readers seeking to understand consciousness and the purpose of their lives on earth, as well as methods for developing skills to experience the spiritual as a powerful reality in daily life, should find *Connecting Heart With Head* an inspiring and useful resource" **Authorhouse - Editoral Assesment Report.**

A Message
John – Roger, D.S.S.
New York Times # 1 Bestselling Author.
THE BOOK THAT INSPIRED
THE MAJOR MOTION PICTURE
"Spiritual Warrior"

"When you have experience with God,
you will realize that God is existence, and in reality,
you don't live God, as much God lives you."

**"So remember that what has been written in
this book here is unknown to you and you can't
trust the unknown. You can have a sort of faith
in it,, a sort of hope in it, a sort of belief in it,
but you cannot yet trust it until you do it and it
works." Spiritual Warriors are always looking
for challenges to take them to next level.**

PREFACE

This book is an attempt to share with you the principles of the process I have learned and to teach you how you can apply these principles in your own life, whatever your circumstances.

Since I am a practical man, this is a practical book. Each chapter is laid out with compassion, caring, and earnestness to share about the Spirit. I believe it is sure to be a valuable reference and resource for those seeking greater understanding of themselves and their relationship with the spiritual worlds, both within and without.

Over the thirty-five years, I have read many books written about this approach to life which have addressed certain aspects of the process. In this book you have the opportunity to read how one man's experience can touch humanity.

I urge you to use what works for you and let go what does not, I apply this principle to my entire life.

As a final word of preparation before you begin to read the first chapter may I offer one brief suggestion which may provide a clue by which the 'secret' may be recognized?

It has been said that there are no heroes these days. But that would be incorrect because no one said we had to be perfect.

Try to personify a quality or qualities like: Intention, Impeccability, Ruthlessness, Dedication, Commitment, Discipline, Focus, Acceptance, Cooperation, Understanding, Empathy, Surrender, Health, wealth, Happiness, Prosperity, Abundance, Riches, Loving, Caring, Sharing, and Touching, and you too, will attain the mental of the Spiritual Warrior. I promise.

Mushtaq Jaafri

San Dimas, CA - 2017

A WORD FROM THE AUTHOR

The information I share here may seem somewhat abstract. If you don't fully understand it at your first reading, that's okay; it took me more than thirty-five years to receive it and then reflect on it—and it took another few more years to validate it. Once I did understand the full significance of **Connecting Heart with Head**, it hit me like the jolt of lightening. **Wham!**

It suddenly dawned on me that we use the **'energy of the heart'** because our heart is the *center of this gut feelings* and closely **connected** with our guidance and inner experience of **who you are as** *a Soul and as a one* with God in your daily life **not in theory but a living reality.**

We also use the structure in our brain **called the pineal gland of the brain** which is commonly known as the "third-eye" or the inner-eye. The 'third-eye' is nothing more nor less than a symbolic connection we already have with the Higher Mind or the Higher Source (or whatever you want to call it) as a Soul and as a one with God not in theory but as a living reality in daily life.

The only reason why we might not be experiencing it because of the too much *'mental-chatter'* that goes on within our minds. This incessant, compulsive thinking of the mind is **what holds u**s back actually from experiencing that connection with the Higher Source.

So— the very first step to making your everyday life magical is to recognize that this connection is already there and we are already connected to it all we need to do is to focus on it and open the 'third-eye' and activate the pineal gland of the brain.

The idea is that the pineal gland which is inside the human brain (also known as the third-eye), once we open up that 'third-eye' it's like the intention goes away as if there is no more two eyes (closed eyes) and that is when the third-eye is activated. What happens next is that we start to observe the mind-activity without being involved in it. It is as if the mind is dead (so to speak) or there is no mind at all.

We begin to realize that we are not the mind. That is why your mind is your enemy because it will go against you in your attempts to opening the 'third-eye' and activating the pineal gland. And, it seems to win because although your Spirit, the Soul is a divine part of God, the mind is the physical armored warrior (so to speak) who will attempt to destroy any chance of ever opening the 'third-eye' and activating the pineal gland of the brain. Our minds play devil's advocate in the Soul, the minds are our enemy.

We should accept them **not** as a victim no matter what is happening. Mind is this thing inside of us that stops us from opening the third-eye and activating it so that we can know what is going on.

Mind is the one that stops us from knowing *who we are and knowing where our true home is in Spirit and go thee in consciousness and become one with God while still living in this physical body.* I habitually use this structure in my brain for my visualization.

I imagine that it is just there, it is called the pineal gland or the third-eye. This is m*y inner-eye that sees everything*. It is actually the structure in my brain that can and does receive the bright, beautiful and divine LIGHT, and it *is* responsible for so many vital processes in the body. If you learn to connect the heart with the head, you will find that this process through the 'energy of the heart' actually helps you h*eal* yourself. You make everyday life magical by opening the 'third-eye'.

CHAPTER 1

Knowledge of the Creation by God.

When I was born in this world, I must have sacrificed a Spiritual World. In the Spiritual World in which I lived as Spirit, as Pure love and as a divine part of God.

I must have looked down into this physical world, and looking from that high pure love, I imagined doing everything with perfect love, because from the place I was looking from, everything looked perfect.

The funny thing is that everything here on earth is still perfect just the way I saw it from the high pure love on the spiritual world above.

Everything here on earth, indeed is still perfect just the way I saw it from the Spiritual world, the problem is that I just don't like it the way it is. So, the problem is not that the physical world is not perfect. The problem is that I need to

1

see it through the eyes of the Spirit. We see the physical world through the two physical eyes and not through the spiritual-eyes (the third-eye) which is often closed due to the lack of not knowing how to open it and activate the pineal gland.

Let me tell you my story of how I might have decided to be born here on earth in this physical body. I believe I must have decided to leave the **realm of Spirit in heaven** in order to gain the experience of the rich living in this physical world and become a Co-creator with God in heaven.

I wanted to experience all levels and conditions of God. Thus, the earth experience is a part of my evolution into the consciousness of God. So, I agreed to be born in the physical realm, but the problem was that to be born in the physical world, I was to be born in the physical body in the Physical realm in order to move down from the positive Spirit realm into the negative five realms namely: *etheric, mental, causal, astral, and of course the physical.*

The point I am trying to convey here is that The Soul, as rule is both male and female, but when I decided to be born into this physical world, I choose to come into this world this time as a male. Also, soul, in itself is both positive and negative, not in the sense it is 'good' or 'bad' but, in the sense of the positive and negative polarity of the battery.

It is complete in its energy pattern, like the Creator is complete. To make the long story of my birth short, as Soul, I first picked up an *etheric* body in the human consciousness below the soul ream in the realms of Spirit.

(This was the very first stage of my human consciousness). I'm still a divine part of Spirit but not as a physical body as yet. Next I descended and picked up a mental body which covered my soul but still not in the physical form. I then picked up the *Causal* and the *Astral* bodies in the same manner and then after up to nine months of stay as a Spirit (in essence) in the body of my mother, I ultimately picked up my own unique *Physical body* all wrapped-up in my own Soul ready to experience the rich living on earth as a human being. The sad thing is that you and I forget that we as human beings, don't really belong here spiritually. You and I were implanted (so to speak) here in this physical body and on this physical world attempting to fulfill certain God-like qualities within ourselves, and we forget that you and I do have a prime directive; **You and I are here to find out who we are, and to find out where our home in Spirit from where we came and to where we return is, and to go there in consciousness, and to have a co- creative consciousness with our Creator God!**

Connecting heart with head in the way I use here is simply means that as Soul, in my own human physical body, not only I as a Soul, through the human form can experience all the negative realms (etheric, mental, casual, astral and the physical), but I also can directly experience the positive (Soul and Spirit) that exist beyond the negative.

The first of the positive realm is the Soul realm. The point is that this is the very first level where I am consciously **aware of my own true nature.**, my true 'beingness' and my **oneness with God**. There are many ascending realms of pure Spirit above the Soul realm. I pretend that Connecting Heart with Head is a symbolic way of my own relationship with the Creator God, where heart represent the Spirit and the head represents the Soul. I sometimes indulge in my own imagination to see what kind of a place this world would be in which to live if everyone on earth could learn to open the third-eye and activate the pineal gland.

As God is my witness, when I do my daily meditations, I imagine connecting my heart in my physical body with the pineal gland in my brain in my head, and it connects me to the Higher Mind or the Higher Source (or whatever you want to call it). I imagine that there is a door at the center of my chest that opens-up and suddenly the bright, beautiful, divine LIGHT enters through my heart center and travels up through my spine where the LIGHT meets with the pineal gland—the inner-eye and, the inner-eye directs that LIGHT through the area of the third-eye in my forehead and travels out into the whole universe. So, the internal becomes the external and it makes my everyday life magical in the truest spiritual sense. I really feel the sensation, the tingle of 'heart-energy' traveling though my beings.

The most amazing part of this connection is that the heart actually helps me heal myself of all the physical ailments and I begin to see the world as a happy place. I see others as divine beings, and see everything inner connected.

Just think of it! I acknowledge my own Spirit's presence by allowing *It* into my own life without restriction or conditions.

I sense as if Spirit touches my heart and wants to heal me now. I am always ever ready to receive of the Spirit at any time and at all times. I believe from the bottom of my heart that a great deal of stress, struggles, sorrows, fear and doubts is a result of not ***knowing how to connect our heart with head***. We let the mind keeps us totally occupied with the past or the future.

I believe that it is the cause of so many of our troubles. You and I can't see the Soul's presence because Soul is 'wrapped-up' in the **five negative** realms of Spirit inside of us. I always tell myself that *Soul is who I am*. Soul is a divine part of *who God Is*. Soul keeps me alive, not the mind. Mind cannot be trusted because mind is the devil's advocate.

I am an extension of the Spirit and, as such, I've certain attributes in common with the Spirit—and not with the mind. *Mind is my enemy* because it will go against me in my Spirit. But, let me be perfectly honest with you and tell you that **connecting heart with dead** is a twenty-four-hours-a-day, seven-days-a-week job. There are no vacations either, but the rewards are certainly worth it.

For thirty—five long years I've been totally committed to *honesty, truth, duty and love*, and a continual demonstration of those efforts. It wasn't easy, at least at first. But, after a while the rewards started coming in and I found **I wouldn't have any other way**. I created love, harmony, happiness, peace, these qualities began to be returned to me

CHAPTER 2

"Connecting Heart with Head."

The point I'm try so hard to convey here is that: **Are we paying attention to the connection? Are we feeling the intuition? Are we focus on it?** A lot of time we tend to be more focus on seeing through the physical eyes rather than through the spiritual eyes.

What I've found is that just as we need the physical eyes to see the physical world, the very same way, we need the spiritual eyes to see the spiritual worlds. Ever notice that whenever you go to see the 3-D movies, they ask you to wear special glasses to see it?

The reason is that wearing these special new glasses allows you to *shut-off the physical eyes* (so to speak) so that you can see the object in front of you with the new special glasses.

This helped me become more aware of the fact that if I put my *intention* on the idea of the intuitive part of my brain (pineal—gland in the head), or the intuitive part of how I see things, perhaps then, I can tap-into the *connecting heart with head* by *feelings* rather than by just thinking so much and rather than reacting so much to the incessant, compulsive, useless, and repetitive thinking of the mind that occupies us 24/7, seven days a week, 365 days a year after year until the end which is death. Just think of it!

For the past thirty-five years, what I have found it that if I control my own 'mind- activity' and not react negatively to emotions (Mind is both thinking and emotions) then, I begin to tap-in and have more ability to tap-in to connect with that Source or connection or God. The good news is that the connection with the Source is *already* there.

What I have discovered is that the one easy way to get rid of all the blocks to the opening of the third-eye and activating the pineal gland of the brain for the connection of heart with head is that I just *observe* the mind-activity without being involved in it. In all honesty, when I first discovered this universal truth about the working of the human mind that I can stop the mind just by *observing* self-talk or mind-chatter or its internal endless dialogues, I thought it was too simplistic to be practical. I remember that I almost threw the book out of the window. (By the way, the book I'm referring to is: **Spiritual Warrior).**

I said to myself: Sure, Just Observe the mind's thinking, and it will all go away. So, I decided to go ahead with the plan just to prove it wrong. But, I must say, I could not prove it wrong.

I noticed, with profound interest that the moment I started to deliberately monitor my own thoughts, all thoughts began very slowly began to subside and lo and behold, eventually leave the mind. I was dumbstruck to say the least. Needless to say, that for the next thirty-five years, that is exactly what I did.

To my utter amazement, soon I was able to take full and complete possession of my own mind 24/7, seven-days a week, 365 days a year after year until now this very moment I am typing these words on my computer to validate my experience for those who are ready to prove me wrong (which you won't).

I was so intrigued by the simplicity of controlling the mind just by monitoring its thinking that I wrote and self-published a book: *How to deliberately Monitor You Thinking?* (available at www.amazon.com). The point is that when I let go of the 'mind-activity' I noticed with profound interest that I reached the point where I could sense the **tiny spot** in back of my head in my brain called the 'third-eye'.

To sum-up everything, the key to remember is this: *Connecting heart and head* is a spiritual connection that is *already* there. It's not about me having to re-establish it. It's more about just opening the third-eye and activating pineal gland of the brain in the head. Back in the East, from where I come from, there are some people, just average people like you and I, who spend a life-time doing daily meditation sessions in an effort to open the third-eye and activate the pineal gland of the brain in the head to meet the 'heart-chakra' and attempt to have the 'heart-energy', travel through the area of the third-eye out toward the universe.

This way, the internal become external. I have seen people who sit on the floor, with eyes closed and legs folded and hand palms resting on the lap.

They meditate for hours and hours at a time, apparently in a blissful mental state as if seeing or hearing or finding something or someone. I often wondered that what is it that these spiritual people see or hear or find inside of the head that keeps them there for such a long time doing the meditations. I know I've hard time sitting doing meditations for just 20 minutes at a time. It's not uncommon for me to look at my watch once in a while.

So—I really wanted to know what is it that keeps these people meditating for many hours at a time. People who have spent a long time in daily meditations say that "whenever, we withdraw our intention inside our heads behind the two eyes and concentrate on the tiny dot there to see a third-eye which opens-up to the Spiritual worlds beyond the physical world." Spiritual Masters of all ages who have spent a life-time in spiritual pursuits affirm that they visualize and *imagine* themselves (not just looking at themselves) **but imagine themselves** traveling in these realms.

These spiritual masters say that they imagine themselves traveling from the physical, to the astral, to the causal, mental, etheric realms of Spirit. These are the negative realms of spirit within the body.

Above the etheric realm of spirit is the very first positive realm of Spirit, **called the Soul realm**. They say that there seems to be a 'gap-of-no-realms' between the lower negative realms of spirit and first positive realm of spirit.

And, to help aid in our travel from the lower negative realm (etheric) to the first positive realm (Soul), a mystical traveler consciousness appears who guides

them and takes them to the Soul realm of Spirit and beyond into the heaven.

All those who have experienced traveling into these lower negative realms of Spirit and gone beyond into higher positive realms of Spirit intuitively agree with the legitimacy of the both the lower and the higher spiritual realms of spirit. To be honest, nothing has influenced my own life than the knowledge and knowing that divine creation by GOD is split into two parts: the lower and the higher planes. The lower planes are a material realm of time, matter, space, and energy, and the physical plane, of course belongs here.

The higher planes are beyond time and space: the true worlds of God. I habitually try my best to travel into these spiritual planes during my meditation sessions. I visualize, or imagine, or just pretend that the lower planes below the Soul plane (physical, astral, causal, mental and etheric) are a 'training-ground' for my self-Realization.

Likewise; the higher planes from the Soul plane and above (there are twenty-one) are the 'training-ground' **for God-Realization. My spiritual goal is to reach the higher planes during my meditation session and connect heart with head.**

The funny thing is that when I am on the higher planes of spirit, I really become aware of myself as a Soul and as a one with God, not in theory but a truly living reality in my daily life.

You might say that I am here on the planet earth to find out who I am and to find out where the Soul plane is and to go there to have a co—creative consciousness with my creator God. This is my whole purpose on this planet.

Perhaps that is why, I love to travel in the higher spiritual planes in my visualization and imagination. I do know, for a fact that I really don't have to die to inherit (so to speak) the Kingdom of Heaven. I *can* have it while I am alive, right—here, right-now! I sometimes imagine that I am **heir to the throne** because I am a divine part of God—and as such I do have all the essence of God within me. I now have reached the consciousness where I say, *"Look God, whatever I can do for you, I am going to do it. I'm doing the best I can. You promised that if I remember you here on the physical world, then, you too will remember me in the spiritual world."*

I know that there is no urgency in Spirit because Spirit has infinite patience for Souls to come home in heaven. I also acknowledge Spirit's presence by allowing it into my life without any conditions or hinder or restrictions. My only job is to be ready to receive the Spirit at any time and at all times because I want the healing from the **'heart-energy'** now.

Yes, I am going to do my job, but let me say this, that I've had it here,. So—anytime you can get me on the Soul plane, and on the other realms of Spirit, let's go (God). For God's sake, please help me, God! I know, that God did not put me here to be a beggar, nor, did God, simply, put me here on earth and said: that's it. **God loves me!**

CHAPTER 3

"Spiritual Beings Having Physical Experience"

Spiritual Masters of all ages who consistently and consciously spend more of their time in spiritual pursuits instead of **reacting to the mind always remain at peace** regardless of what is happening in the material world.

They know that as human beings, *we can never ever control God*, but we can most certainly 'align' and *flow* with God's Will. **In fact, I was so intrigued with this truth that I wrote and self-published a book: Go With The Flow**—referring to the above statement.(available at: www.authorhouse.com). Speaking for myself, I start each day by reading a passage from this remarkable book, *Go With the Flow*. Each passage provides me *a focus for my awareness* as a Soul and a one with God not, just in theory but, a daily living reality in my own life. Its amazing how well each passage helps me move along my *intention*. Then, at the end of that day, just before I retire I read the very same passage again and then write a passage, or two about my experience in my daily journal for future reference. For more information about my story, please log on to my new website: www.gowiththeflowstory.com.

The point I am trying to convey here is that in the final analysis we as human beings are truly a spiritual beings having a physical experience here on earth. So—the next logical question is: **how do we go about experiencing the awareness of ourselves as spiritual being while still living in this physical body?** The answer is simply this:

By *Connecting* the heart –energy with the 'third-eye' the Pineal-gland of brain.For me, the best time to connect the heart-energy with the head is first thing the morning and at night just before going to sleep. I start my meditation by taking a few deep breath, relaxing, I sit straight my feet on the floor.

Then I withdraw my intention within to the pineal gland of my brain inside my head. I visualize or just imagine that there is a door in front of my chest. I imagine this door opening and the bright, beautiful, divine LIGHT entering from into the heart-center in my chest to the pineal gland in the brain in my head.

Then, I visualize that this heart-energy traveling through the spine in my back meets the third-eye (pineal gland) inside my head and *the third-eye directs the heart-energy outside to the whole universe through the forehead which is the third-eye area.*

So—the internal becomes the external. The key to the success of this meditation is that I imagine the pineal gland in the brain is *a tiny red dot, or black dot, or even a purple dot* in the size of about one of my full physical eye.

This makes it easier for me to let my body know just where I am addressing my own intention in my head to make a *connection* with my heart-energy. *Just as the brain generates electro magnet waves (brain waves), the human heart also generates the electro magnet energy (heart-waves).* The only difference is that the heart-waves are a thousand times more powerful than the brain-waves.

But, when we connect the heart with the head these combines electro—magnet-energy of both is very powerful. I often feel a tingle or a sensation or pressure in my head and I know that my third-eye is beginning to open and activate the pineal gland in my head. I can literally feel the bright, beautiful LIGHT traveling through my body. I never get tired of this wonderful sensation in my head.

For me, seeing the tiny purple dot, in the size of my full eye behind the eyebrows gives me the legitimacy and the proof of my own ability to open the third-eye and activate the pineal gland in my brain.

To make the vision of opening my third-eye even more vivid and clear, I close my eyes. The point I am trying to make is the pineal gland of brain (third-eye) is *structure inside the brain in your head that sees everything and receives the bright, beautiful LIGHT from the heart that heals **everything in your body***. I acknowledge this process of the Spirit within my body.

I accept Spirit's presence in my body and work with it without any restrictions. I let it touch me because I want the healing now, not last week, or in a month or a year. My job is to be ever-ready to be healed by the Spirit.

It's amazing how well the Spirit has always healed all of my physical ailments without my knowledge. Please understand that I don't claim to be a more special, more gifted, or more spiritual person than you. I'm just like you. And, that is the truth. I just connect my heart with head as often as possible.

I'm a spiritual being having a physical experience here on earth. I've become aware of myself as a Soul and as a one with God not, in theory but a living reality in my daily life.

This book is an attempt to share the process of connecting the heart with head. I know the process works, because I have tried and tested this process time and time again in my own life.

Since I consider myself somewhat a practical man, you too will find that this is a practical book. This book has helped me literally live an inner spiritual life in a constantly changing, challenging and mostly demanding material world. All I ask is to use what works for you and to let go of what doesn't work for you.

CHAPTER 4

Accepting Mind as an Enemy

A spiritual master I was working with once asked me: Can you accept an enemy and say: "I love you?" I often heard him say to others that: "I love you if you love me. And, I love you if you kill me."

These are very powerful statements. I really didn't understand the true meaning of what the master was saying. Then, suddenly, it dawned on me that once I truly embrace the enemy, it turns to help me. Then I don't have stubbornness, I have determination.

This transformed the moment I accepted it, and all the power that was blocking me before now becomes of ascension, of uplifting. The master taught me that once I accept the enemy and once I embrace it, that enemy will transform and yield its power to me. Then, the master said: "I'm referring to accepting the enemy within—which is your own mind."

He said; your own thoughts, your emotions, and your feelings will shake you harder than anyone else can shake you. That is why your own mind is your enemy because it will go against you in your Spirit.

And, it seems to win because although your Spirit, the Soul is the Spiritual warrior, the mind is the physical armored warrior who will attempt to destroy any chance of ever spending more time in your spiritual pursuits and make you re-act to material world.

You will find dealing with all 'petty-tyrants" in your daily life, bugging you with impurity. So be sure to identify the petty-tyrants in your own life, past or present. Some of our spouses and kids seemed to be expert in this field. They will hit your hot-buttons.

The key to all this is **observing** your own thoughts instead of reacting, or fighting them during your meditation. I **observe** the thoughts that come into my mind. I notice that the more I **observe** my own thought in my mind, the more they begin to subside and eventually leave the mind.

For me one easy way to open that pineal gland of my brain and activate it for connecting the **heart with head** is to sit in an easy chair. I take a few deep breaths, and focus on my own breathing and as I begin to do that I begin to put the awareness more within—as an **observer mode r**ather than an reactive mode. When I am in that meditation, I just **observe** the thoughts that come in. I don't judge them as good or bad, happy or unhappy, or resist them. I just continue to **observe** them.

The funny thing is that the more I **observe** them they begin to go away from the mind naturally almost as I am not fighting them. The reason all thoughts begin to go away is because I am not giving them energy.

And, as those thoughts begin to go away and then I focus on relaxing my eyes, my face.

Then, I close my eyes and when I close my eyes I begin to raise my brain waves from the beta level to the alpha level where my own mind start to generate mostly more *alpha* waves, more **relaxing** waves in the pineal gland of my brain and I am shutting-off (so to speak) my two physical eyes, and opening my spiritual-eye (third-eye). Then, with my own two eyes closed,

I begin to focus moving my eyes almost *up looking at my forehead* behind the eyebrows. I am looking at the imaginary third-eye in the size of my full eye, on my forehead. I see totally darkness there and lo and behold, a tiny purple dot appears and I know that my **third-eye is in** the process of opening and activating the pineal gland in the brain.

The point I am trying to convey here is that as I close my physical eyes, and look upward into the dark area of my forehead behind the eye brows, what I am symbolically doing is doing is that I am literally putting my focus on the third-eye which is closed at the moment and then I decide that as I am putting the intention on the closed third-eye—it suddenly opens-up and I do this over and over again until someday, it does open up for me.

Most people claim that with persistence and patience and practice it does open-up. The only question is that how much you want it to open-up and how much practice with persistence you are willing to do it.

And, as I do that I begin to put the awareness within and begin to experience the connection with the higher source to which I am connected already. For me, this experience, this awareness, this connecting heart with head comes as a sensation, as a tingle or some kind of pressure in my head. It is something visual, or feeling inside my head and as I begin to do that I begin to tap-in to more of that energy, more of that connection that already exists now—but cluttered up by the reactive mind. How long, then, it takes to learn to open the

third-eye and activate the pineal gland in the brain? It depends upon you.

If you love and trust in God, then you'll find the process to be an easy skill to master. All it takes is to observe the mind—activity without being involved in it. Spiritual masters of all ages call observation the key to letting go. When something unpleasant, something disturbing shows up, and you just begin to observe it without reacting emotionally to it, you will notice with profound interest that you don't ever get thrown off balance. Only human beings are capable of observing the presence of God in all things including us.

Recently, I did a Google-search for How to Open the Third-eye and Activate the Pineal Gland. To my surprise and amazement, more than 512,000 hits showed up on this particular Google-search. I even found the internet loaded with spiritual people offering techniques how to open the third-eye and activate the Pineal gland of the brain.

Apparently; this is exact the kind of information people who are spiritual and not necessarily religious were looking for. You see, religious is traditions and rituals *we do.* Spiritual is something *we are.* There is a difference because you can be a very religious person, and not be spiritual—and vice versa.

Spiritual Masters of all ages who have spent a life-time in spiritual pursuits instead of reacting to the material world affirm that we as human beings are a spiritual beings having a physical experience here on earth. We are SPIRIT—a divine part of God. We are the essence of who God Is. Just think of it!

The funny thing is that many spiritual people are offering various techniques how to quickly and safely open the third-eye and activate the Pineal gland of the mind. Some of these Google-searches have several millions hits on the Google-search. It does prove to me, at least to my own satisfaction anyway, that we as a human race are ready and willing to accept that we are not here to do what we know how to do. We are not here just to learn what we already know.

We are here to learn what we do not know and what we do not know how to do which is I believe, learning to open the third-eye and activate the Pineal gland of the brain to find out who we are and to find out where the Soul realm is and to go there to have a co-creative consciousness with God in heaven. This is the way how I see our existence here.

What I mean is that we don't belong here—spiritually! Perhaps, that is why we have such a hard time fulfilling our spiritual promise here on earth and making ourselves do what we want to do according to our intention, because our intention only works best in the Spirit.

I earnestly believe from the bottom of my own heart, that our creator has given each human being three special and unique gifts that no other creation by God has been given. I call these three gifts from God the *awareness of inner spiritual movement* because they allow me to **observe** the presence of God in all things, including myself.

Human beings are sacred because of the three gifts from our creator. If only we could understand that simple fact, we would never need to read another self-help book! How can we **observe** God when we are observing outside where it can never be found. All spiritual teachings say: **The kingdom of heaven is within**. The Bible it says: "Seek first the kingdom of Heaven:

So—what are those three special and unique gifts that every human have? You may ask: My answer. The first gift is the **intention.** I mean, we as human beings have the God-given power and the privilege to put our intention wherever we want to. The second gift is *concentration*. We can put our concentration on anything or anyone or anywhere we want to. **Please remember that I don't mean focus, but concentration because there is a difference. Focus is just to see or look.**

Concentration is going beyond focus. It the separation of thinking of the mind and y**our awareness of the mind's thinking without being any part of the mind's** thinking. In the East, it is called the *awakening process*, or a mind without any thoughts or a no-mind. It proves that we are *not* the mind. We are Spirit—a Soul.

The third gift is the **imagination**. None of the creation by God has been given this special and unique gift of imagination. The power of imagination is awesome and is responsible for the comforts and making everyday life magical, to say the least.

The sad thing is that we, as a human race, have advanced enormously technologically, but as a race we are still doing the same destructive things that were reported in the biblical days thousands of years ago. I believe that although, we have advanced tremendously in the material world, we are still in the 'stone—age' spiritually.

I believe human race is shifting in consciousness now where we are ready and willing to open the third-eye and activate the Pineal gland in the brain to make a connection with the higher Mind, or Higher Source (or whatever you want to call it). My Google-search proved this fact, at least to my own satisfaction. As I go about my daily business, I try to put my own *intention* inside my head on the Pineal gland in my brain (third-eye). I concentrate on the third-eye—area on my forehead behind the eyebrows. Using the power of *imagination* I then, imagine that there is a 'door' on the center on my chest that opens-up, and I visualize, or imagine or just pretend that the bright, beautiful, divine LIGHT, enter my heart—and travel through my back spine upward in my head and meets the 'third-eye' which direct the heart-energy through the third-eye-area of the forehead and browse outside the whole universe and the internal becomes the external and I sense as if I've become aware of myself as a Soul and as a one with God not just in theory but a living reality in my daily life. ***It takes me just two minutes to do it. I d***o this meditation as often as I can and anywhere and anytime I can. Just think of it Anytime, I am stuck on the freeway traffic waiting for it move forward, guess, **what do you think I do** Yeah—you guessed it. I take a few deep breaths. I put my intention on the 'third-eye' I concentrate on it. I imagine the door in the center of my chest opening and the bright, beautiful, divine Light entering through my spine and meeting the third-eye which directs the heart-energy through third-eye are behind the eyebrows outside the universe and connects with the universal mind or the source for experiencing myself as a Soul and as a one with God as a living, breathing reality in the world. I do the same meditation if I am sitting alone in my car for a long time wait my family to do shopping or whatever. I do this meditation 24/7 day in and day out.I've now reduced my own life to just one thing: Seeking God 24/7. I do this through a process I learned from my spiritual teacher who revealed to me the three gifts of God. The most amazing thing about this quick meditation is that it helps me align myself with God.

This short meditation has revealed to me the **secret** that inside of me who I am as a Spirit meets the Soul who is there temporarily. Here the Spirit, the divine part of who I am meets me. The spiritual masters of all ages calls it 'the point of convergence'. This short meditation has assisted me in converging my spirit back into alignment. My Soul is what keeps me alive, not my mind. Mind as strong as it may sometimes seem to be, is just vehicle for connecting heart with head. Mind can be constructive if used rightly but it can be very destructive if used wrongly. Mind is the enemy within and I accept it as such. Accepting the enemy within in the way I use here refers to the two aspects of the left and the right sides of the spirit. Our mind plays a devil's advocate in the left side of the spirit.

Finally, let me say this that one of the most powerful thing opening the third-eye and activating the Pineal gland of the brain is to look more deeply at *who I am* and w*hat I am about.* I take some time to look within myself and see *who* *is there*— and become with it. I've truly found the true **me**, and I am truly living that life.

What's more I really don't care whether I live or die because that part of me will never die and always exists. You might say that I live from the outside in. Doing my daily meditations, I've been able to open up sort of a passageway between my Soul and the Spirit by opening the third-eye and activating the Pineal gland of my brain. I always try to catch myself thinking. You might say I've become a 'mind—watcher'.

I have spent more than thirty-five long years reading every book that I could lay my hands on, hoping to come to a deeper awareness of God. Like most of the people I know, I too had my own preconceived ideas of what the Spirit, or the Divine, or God look like. Unfortunately, to my dismay, after spending all these long years in the spiritual pursuits, I discovered that the reality of God cannot be learned through study.

I discovered that the only way I can discovered God is through direct experience inside of me. Spiritual masters of all ages confirm that the Spirit does not care whether you want to align with it now, last week, or in a month—it moves on Its own way and Its own time.

And, my job is be ready to receive the Spirit. Perhaps, that is why the Spirit is ruthless—in a nice way. Spirit does not care where, or when, or how it touches me. But, I can tell you one thing. It is all well worth the wait once the Spirit **did touch me.** For me, one thing is for sure, *God is unknowable—but, I know God!*

Just think of it!

Chapter 5

We Can Only Give What We Have

Not too long ago, I heard a spiritual master tell an amazing true story that **repetition is indeed the mother of all skills**. What that means in plain language is that I can know the Soul through the repetition of my direct experience inside me at which time the information on these pages will move out of the theoretical stage to and become experiential—I guarantee it!

Yes—*repetition is the mother of all skills,* I say this because you may have noticed that I have quiet frequently repeated myself throughout this book in an effort to impress upon your mind the key ideas I want to present to you. So— please remember it's not a typo, or error or some editing mistake or anything else. I believe when you read this amazing story, you, too will agree that why I attempted to repeat myself over and over again—many time, repeating the concept (such as meditation, or Pineal gland) verbatim. This is an amazing story of a spiritual preacher in the Mid-West who had just delivered a most profound, a most powerful, highly motivational and forceful sermon to his congregation during his Sunday church service.

This story proved to me the legitimacy, at least to my own satisfaction, the truth of an old adage: **repetition is the mother of all skills.**

In all fairness, I don't remember the exact words of the story, so I would like to tell you this preacher's story in my own words. One Sunday afternoon, this preacher had given a powerful sermon about: *Higher Consciousness,* "It is, in essence, the preacher said, a way or path to God."

"Higher Consciousness is the way, the only way to God", he said, and furthermore the surest way to God is to let God take over your Soul; open yourself to God constantly, to let God's wisdom, and love and truth to God's effect.

"What that means in plain language", he said, "is that the mind must disappear so that the Soul can transcend into the higher realms of Spirit and liberated for perfect freedom so that Soul literally withdrawn from the physical body and travel into the higher Pure realms of Spirit for God-realization."

The preacher continued, *"Not only can the Soul, through the human form, experience the lower (physical, astral, causal, mental and etheric) realms of Spirit, but it also can experience the higher (Pure Spirit, divine Spirit) realms of Spirit.*

The inborn goal of the Soul is to become explorer of the rich living on earth displaying love for all things—and at all times—and doing the things that trap us—to God." The preacher said that we may not be worthy of anything— but we are indeed **worthwhile** to God as a Soul.

The Preacher emphasized the fact that the division between the two sides of the Spirit is so delicate, that for the majority of the human population, it can take many years of inner-knowing and experience to finally find the subtle heart-energy emanating from the two sides of the Spirit to connect with the head and travel outside into the universe from within.

I can say 'amen' to that because it took me more than thirty-five years of experience to learn to recognize the deeper awareness of God through my direct experience with Higher Consciousness, or Spirit, or God. The funny thing is that when I did find God (as an inner awareness) I wasn't floating through the air saying: "Whoo, whoo, whoo, whoo, whoo I got it!

Anyway, let's get back to the story. The preacher closed his sermon by emphasizing again about the importance of Soul's permanent relationship with God in our daily lives and seeing our being as a spiritual being having a physical experience here on earth. I cannot say his exact words because his sermon was so spell bounding experience.

This preacher has indeed given his congregation the most powerful sermon he had ever given in his career as a preacher and a reverend of that church. Everyone in the church applauded, cheered, and some even cried with joy by listening to his sermon and were truly lifted to a higher level of mental and spiritual elevation.

The next Sunday afternoon service this preacher gave the very same sermon verbatim, and sure enough, the whole church congregation once again applauded, cheered, and cried, while listening to every word the preacher was saying with passion and conviction. You couldn't hear a pin drop. It was so quiet. You could sense his love and devotion to his sermon. People in the church were so spellbound again like before.

Then, the following Sunday, the preacher again talked about the exact same *Higher Consciousness* sermon, verbatim. And, this went on for another few more weeks. The story goes that after a few more weeks of listening to the same very sermon word-for-word, the elders of the church along with the board of directors of the church, began to worry and became somewhat anxious wondering what is going on with this preacher and whether he had lost his sermons, or perhaps his mind or something. So—one day some of the church elders and the directors of the church went to see him at his home and said: *Reverend Jackson you have been preaching the very same sermon word-for-word.*

The Reverend replied to the elders and the directors: **"I know that, and I will be giving the very same sermon each week, and am going to be doing that until everyone in the church congregation gets this message implanted in their minds."** I believe that the preacher was trying to prove to the church congregation the universal principle that **repetition is the mother of all skills.**

The more you hear something, the more you understand. And, the more you understand, the more you actually use so that it becomes a reflex and part of your. In Muslim tradition, people pray for five times a day, seven days a week, 365 days a year after year until the end which is death.

During the five times a day prayers, Muslim people repeat the very same prayers word-for-word verbatim over and over again. There are people in the Muslim communities who have memorized the holy Qur'an and repeat it word-by-word. I am only sharing this information to give the legitimacy of the proof of that repetition is the mother of skills. Speaking for myself, I have spent a life-time in repetition of certain sacred words to control my mind. Repetition of these sacred words (called self-suggestions) has helped me control my own mind.

These sacred words (called mantras) kind of squeeze my mind's incessant, compulsive, useless, repetitive and involuntary thinking. I've taken full and complete possession of my own mind 24/7. My own mind would not dare think of something without my permission. Tell me, how many people you know of who can honestly say this. Sure, mind does try to get its own way but, I can bring it back just by observing the mind activity.

For me It's an awakening process which is the separation of the mind and thinking—I call it the awareness of myself as Soul behind the mind's thinking.

Finally, what I am trying to convey here is that if you find that I too, (like the preacher) have repeated myself over and over a again in this book, it is because I want the readers of this book to remember this: *We can only give what we have for ourselves.*

Many people have asked me. "By what authority do I speak?' After all I am not a preacher, or a scholar, or anyone special, or gifted or spiritual. Yet, I could most certainly ask the very same question. "By what authority do you question?'

The funny thing is that the authority to question others and to speak-out are both inherent within each one of us. *I say what I say because I can.* I believe that most people never speak out because they don't trust themselves and are very afraid of what other people may say, think or do and are afraid of their reactions.

Dealing with people what I've discovered is that most people, especially well meaning family members and close friends have a tendency toward becoming a control freaks. **Some kids and spouses are expert in this field.**

When I understood that I cannot have control, then I could surrender to what is in control; God, and let Him continue to run the universe. Sometimes I used to sense God's power, but I somehow felt it as fear and I contracted. But, you know, what? **There is nothing in God to inspire fear. Just think of it!**

The problem usually starts when I believe that I will be alone or abandoned, and that I will lose control of reality.

Once I did make a determined choice for surrendering control to God; I became free in it. Not free *from* it, but free *in* it. I now live in conscious alignment with the Soul.

After spending thirty-five years in spiritual pursuits instead of reacting to the material world, I now do have this truth and I want to give it to the whole world. I've endeavored to live my own life internally, without attachment to the material world.

The thing to remember is that what have you created in the 'karma-actions, that will change the course of your own life and perhaps the course of the whole world.

"It is *not what is happening that is important; what is important is what you are doing with it. Thus the Spiritual Warrior says, Regardless of what it looks like, regardless of what is my perception, I will use everything for my advancement, upliftment, and growth.*: John-Roger – D.S.S.

Chapter 6

God Is Un-knowable
but I Know God

"Your task is to build a better world," Said God, and I answered, "How?" "This world is such a large vast place, and, oh so complicated now, and, I am so small and useless, there is nothing I can do." But God in all his wisdom said, "You just build a better you."

For the past thirty-five plus years I believed that I can use my own mind to find God. Never did I realized the universal truth that the mind has limitations and stops at the limit of the mind. One of my spiritual masters often said: "We are moving from the Unknown to the Unknowable.

Frankly, I had no clue what in the heck it means. Then, suddenly, it hit me like a jolt of lightening.Wham! It really dawned on me what this great spiritual master was telling me. I reasoned that if I know something it is called the *known*, likewise;

if I don't know something, it is called the **unknown** (simple right) but, this unknown can be known. And, finally there is what we can **_never_** know—*the unknowable.* So— what this great spiritual master was telling me was that in order to find God, we are moving from the unknown to the unknowable, because God is in the unknowable.

What I am trying to convey here is that the search for God isn't a race toward a finish line. As for the unknowable, it is true, "God is unknowable, but I know God." How can that true be? How do I recognize God? My answer is: The best I can. I've now reduced my own life to just one thing: *Seeking God 24/7.* I do this through a process I have learned from my spiritual teacher who taught me this.

I call seeking God in every moment of my life as stalking the Spirit. Or consciously show my love for God by repeating a self-suggestion (mantra) *"God is unknowable but, I know God.* I repeat this affirmation 24/7. I also stalk death by rehearsing my last words on my deathbed: *"I did the best I could, God!"*

As I go about my daily business, I say, do and even think what will bring me closer to God regardless of any distractions, or whatever I may have to sacrifice for it. My mind's fundamental purpose is to keep me busy with guilt, doubt, and worries and spinning around on the physical world.

That is why my mind is my own worst enemy because it will always goes against me in my spiritual pursuits. I observe my mind's thinking 27/7. How can I **observe** God when I am observing bad thinking of the mind, guilt, doubt, worry and resentment? I can't because God can only be found in 'goodness'. That is where I find God, goodness in nature, all things living and the universe. People often wonder why do I stalk death while I am still living here on earth.

They ask why do I rehearse my last words, **"I did the best I could, God"?** I say to them because those words might help me stop the wheel of 84 for me. Then, they ask: What in the heck is the wheel of 84? I say: the wheel of 84 means that a soul must pass through rounds of eighty-four *lakhs* of rebirths. In Hindi and Urdu languages a *lakh* means one hundred thousand. So— souls pass through eight-four hundred thousand rounds of birth and death.

Please understand that it is not my intent to give a long dissertation about the legitimacy of the wheel of 84. The modern public libraries are full of the books on this subject. My only purpose here is to show how I may stop the rebirth process for me.

Finally, I will lead you step-by-step through a process I've personally used for moving from the unknown to the unknowable to find God. I've literally experienced everything I am about to share with you. It is a practical way to control the 'mind-activity' 27/7.

The very first step in the process of moving from the unknown to the unknowable to find God to go beyond the limits of the human mind. The human mind, as powerful as it seems to be, it does have definite limits and it stops at the limits, as if the mind is dead or no-mind. You cannot use mind to find God.

The division between the left and the right sides of the Spirit is so delicate that it is hard to recognize the subtle 'alignment' energies emanating from the two sides of the Spirit.

It is very difficult to see where the alignment energies are coming from. These alignment energies don't obey any rules; it was up to me to use them properly to advance my spiritual intention. For me alignment with the Spirit was an ongoing challenge for me. The reason is that for thirty-five plus years,

I didn't even know that the Spirit has two sides, the left side and the right side. Alignment with Spirit involves detachment from the material world; but it doesn't mean to hate the world. The joy of alignment flows into everything.

We must live in alignment through the right side of the Spirit by loving, caring and sharing. We must not live through the left side of the Spirit because our minds play devil's advocate in the left side of the Spiri; that is why the mind is your enemy.

This chapter will assist you in converging your Spirit back into alignment.

My spiritual teacher taught me that alignment does not happen in the known, it comes only in the unknowable and it happens as an *awareness* of unknowable. What I have discovered is that I can come into awareness of the unknowable by coming into alignment with it.

For me, the *awareness* is synonymous with the unknowable. That is why I say: ***God is unknowable—but I know God.*** Very simply stated, 'awareness' is becoming aware of myself as a soul and as a one with God not in theory but a living reality in my daily life.

Know this: when convergence takes place, for most, it is "grace" (me too) Then, we come into alignment once again. The key to remember is this: In the left and the right sides of Spirit, we find the known and the unknown.

Both sides of the Spirit are necessary to maintain balance. (it took me more than thirty-five years to know this). So— what are the two aspects of the Left Side and the Right Side of Spirit? The Left Side of Spirit can be imagined as the Intuitive, Emotional, Creative, Earthly, Dark, Path away from God. The Right Side of spirit can be visualized as Logical, Intellectual, Destructive, Spiritual, LIGHT, Path toward God. Only through the Right Side of the Spirit, can you and I go into the unknowable and have alignment with it.

If you are going into the Left Side of Spirit, you are, in essence going away from the unknowable—God! I must admit that it's not easy to live on this planet, simply because I have to live here, and live here, and live here. And, some part of me says. "I'm tired, Lord." I know for a fact, that only God can release me. I also know that in order to win my freedom from the bondage from this material world, I've first to surrender to the unknowable which is God.

As I go about approaching the unknowable (God) I try my level best that my own 'ego' intention does not move my **awareness** out of alignment into the Left side and get stuck here for eternity.

CHAPTER 7

Question and Answers on the Mind and Soul

This chapter is an attempt to answer the most frequently asked questions about mind, soul and Spirit. Remember that repetition is the mother of all skills, so don't be surprised if you find myself repeating some information.

Q. What does the human mind really look like?

A. I believe that if you ask this question to a hundred people, you'll probably get a hundred different answers and they will all the right in their own ways. I'm going to answer this question in the way it was intuitively given to me through inner guidance over a long period of time. For a long time, I imagined the mind as a five-part entity namely: ***The Conscious mind. The Sub-conscious mind. The gap— of-no-mind. Brain Cells and the Field of Consciousness Region.*** Modern libraries are full with books on the working of the home mind for those who are intrigued by

47

intellectual the study of the human mind. Spiritual masters of all ages who have spent a life-time in spiritual pursuits instead of reacting to the material world confirm that the human mind plays a devil's advocate in the Left Side of the Spirit that's why the mind is our enemy and we should it as such and not as a victim no matter what is happening. The mind works through the five passions—anger, greed, attachment, lust, and vanity. These five passions of the mind will bring hurt to you. Do not let your thoughts move you; let your Spirit and heart move you.

Q. How does the mind become conscious of everything happening on the physical plane?

A. All data or information received by the conscious level of the mind through the five physical senses (sight, sound, smell, taste and touch) is classified and stored in the subconscious level of the mind. It is estimated that ninth-tenth of a person's conscious reaction to daily events, situations and circumstances, from the most trivial to the most major occurrences, are computer-like feedback from the mind.

All of our decisions that we make on a daily basis are usually based upon what we have stored-up in the mind. But, unfortunately, the big problem arises when the mind gets in the way and tries to keep us spinning around in the lower realms of Spirit (physical, astral, causal, mental and etheric) through mind's incessant, compulsive thinking that goes on 24/7. Ever notice, there is a constant, endless dialogue or self-talk, if you will, that is always going on in your own mind without your consent or knowledge? (I'll talk more about this later). The sad thing is that this non-stop thinking of the mind makes most people think that *we are our own mind*. (how sad?). We forget the truth that the mind is just an instrument, a device or an equipment just like computer, that was given to us as a gift from our creator (God) for our Soul to experience all it can while in the human physical body. The main thing to remember is this: *you are not (I do mean not) your own mind.* So— *if you are not any part of your mind, then, you do have the God-given power and the privilege of taking full and complete possession of your own mind and direct to any end you may choose.* As God is my witness, I'm a living proof of that.

Q. If you are not your own mind, then, who are you?

A. Spiritually, speaking, you are **awareness** behind your own thinking of the mind. The moment you can truly recognize, relate, assimilate and apply this secret to your own life, it will come as an awakening process. Many years ago, this first awakening process came into my life as an act of 'grace'. I was sitting in the parking lot of my office building ready a book and suddenly I received my very first **glimpse of the awakening process** which is: *separation of thinking and awareness.* It hit me like a bolt of lightning. It dawned me that that I am in reality, an *awareness* between the thinking of the mind and my **awareness** of the mind's thinking. It gave me the proof positive (at least to my own satisfaction) that I am not my own mind—instead *I'm the observer* (awareness) *behind my thinking—mind.* **For the very first time in my spiritual pursuits, I could see my spirituality through my own physical individuality.** I could truly sense myself as a spiritual being having a physical experience. But, perhaps, the biggest reward of my spending more time in spiritual pursuits instead of material world came that *I literally, became aware of myself as a Soul* (awareness) behind the thinking—mind) *and as one with God—not in theory but a living reality. (Later, I learned from my spiritual master that awakening process was called Soul Transcendence).*

Sure enough, **this act of "grace"** began to assist me in converging my own Spirit back into alignment with my own Soul. **I know what I am talking about is pretty heavy stuff but all those spiritual people who have** intuitively experience the concept called "convergence" know exactly what I am talking about.

Q. How can I bypass the mind and free my Soul?

A An easy way for me has been to try to become aware of your own thoughts 24/7.This will cause them to subside and eventually leave the mind. I call awareness the key to letting go. Only human beings are capable of the awareness of the presence of God in all things, including themselves. Human beings are sacred for that one reason. The challenge for me was that every time, I had made a resolution to become aware of myself as a Soul and as a one with God, the negative power of the mind would come in and challenge me to demonstrate just how much I meant it. In a way, the mind became my enemy and played devil's advocate (so to speak) in my **Left Side of Spirit**. I earnestly believe from the bottom of my heart that it's testing, doubting, holding back were essential in my spiritual growth because they showed to me where I was going; they helped me to define my intention, and they made me work for it. This was the main reason for me to remain contact with the **left and the right** of Spirit to be spiritually whole. *For me to deny one side or the other of the Spirit is to deny part of myself. I try not to follow the left-sided path **which is a path away from God**.* But, understand that you cannot entirely control your own mind. It is just too powerful, and the mind will attempt to destroy you.

However, you can learn to replace the mind's incessant, compulsive thinking with creative, universally inspired thinking using positive affirmations or self—suggestions. I try to keep my own mind so busy with positive affirmations that there is *literally* no time left for the mind to think on its own. **Affirmations and self-suggestions are powerful tools that allow me to control my own mind.**

Finally, let me say this that experiencing myself as a Soul and as a one with God comes when I remember that I am one with God as HE is with me not in theory but a living reality in my own life. How hard is it for the human race to understand it.

What kind of a place this world would be in which to live if all of us did understand it. Sure, we have advanced enormously technologically, but as human race, we are backward millions of years—spiritually.

Q. Can you share a sacred mantra or word I can chant to replace my mind's negative thinking?

A. For over thirty-five years, chanting mantras and the sacred words has enabled me to sort of squeeze the mind's thinking out of the mind and literally replace it with my own mantra and sacred word. I chant ANI-HU in a long drawn out sound.

ANI means empathy, creating empathy and connection with God. HU is an ancient Sanskrit *word* for God. Close your eyes, take a few deep breaths, and chant HUUUUUUUUUUU (pronounced Hue). When chanting ANI-HU in a group it brings the group into greater spiritual attunement to dedicate the group to Spirit.

Q. What is calling-in-the Light mean?

A. Calling-in-the Light is a *form* of a prayer where we are trying to bring ourselves into oneness with God for the highest good of all. There is no right or wrong way of Calling in the Light, Even the words are not so important. What matters is the *loving and devotion* with which it is done. We call for the Light with perfect love and perfect understanding, keeping in mind our true destinies on this planet. We don't belong here—*spiritually!* We are engrafted into the body.

Q. How many brain cells are in a human cerebral cortex?

A. Napoleon Hill, in his book *Think and Grow Rich* says: estimated that there are some 24 billion brain cells in the human cerebral cortex. What's most amazing is the new found theory that human brain has two parts: the left-brain and the right-brain. The working of the human brain is somewhat complex but the key to remember is that the human brain isn't the mind; instead, it is the individual, an active entity of the mind that allows the Light to reach from the heart and connect to the Pineal gland of the brain (called the third—eye) in the head. Visualizing opening the third-eye really activate all your psychic senses when we use the energy of the heart, because the heart is the center of our gut-feelings and intuition, and is closely connected to your guidance to your psychic powers.

Q. What is the Pineal gland of the brain?

A. Pineal gland is a small structure in your own brain, you can imagine for visualization purpose that it is just there. This is your 'inner-eye' This is the 'eye' that sees **everything**. Actually this is the structure that can and does receive the LIGHT, and its responsible for so many vital processes in the mind. So—when we actually put our intention, on to that Pineal gland, we can imagine that as a really simple dot, a red dot, a black dot or a purple dot You can even imagine as full size eye—just the size of your eye inside your head, we call it the Pineal gland, so that it's easier to kind of let our body know that where we are directing your intention. The funny thing is that for me, visualizing the Pineal gland helps me **Connect** my **heart with head, helps** and converge my Spirit back into alignment—again!

Q. Where is the Third-eye area and how to open it?

A. Your third-eye area is right above your eyebrows. One easy way to open the 'third-eye' is to just imagine that there is a door that can center over your chest that opens up and **this bright, beautiful, divine LIGHT** enters through the heart center and travels up the spine, where it meets the Pineal gland of the brain, with that third-eye, and the inner-eye directs that LIGHT through your **third-eye-area** out into the universe, so the internal becomes the external.

The key to successful opening of the third-eye and activating the Pineal gland of the brain is to feel the sensation of the LIGHT traveling to heart. *Heart actually helps you to heel yourself* and you see the world through the inner-eye. So—just feel the heart and head connection. When you do this process through heart-energy you see the world as a happy place. You see other people as divine beings because everything is really inner connected that is what I call a way for blissful living.

So—I say keep your third-eye open as much as possible, engage your heart chakra because it connects your heart with head. The exercise will assist you to open your heart center for your intuition and your inner guidance and the life becomes magical. I use this visualization technique every single day and it takes me just two minutes to do it. Spiritual masters of all ages who spent a life-time in spiritual pursuits instead of reacting to the material world say that there are going to be times when you are forced by your events, circumstances or situations or daily happening to look more deeply at who you are and what you are about. Take time to look within yourself, see who you in there through the inner meditation.

Q. What is the Wheel of 84?

A. Spiritually speaking. When our ego clashes with another ego, they both want to be right and win. Let's say that person becomes so angry, so frustrated and outraged to the extent that he or she kills (perhaps accidently) another person then, the law of cause and effect says that person's act must be repaid in another life to balance this cause. The point is that we are as human beings, on earth, in this physical body are held accountable to whatever we do, say and even just think that is not for the highest good of all. We will be held accountable for whatever pain or sorrows or sufferings (no matter how justified) to inflict upon others; causing a need for rebirth to balance our bad acts whether we like it or not. Spiritual masters of all ages has confirmed that when we were born in this world we did agree with our Creator God. But, unfortunately, as we know quite well, that things do not always here on earth go the way we want to, or the way we existed in the spiritual world where we existed as spirit, as pure love and everything was perfect. So, therefore, we say it is not perfect here on earth. But, as a matter of scientific truth, every here in the material world is perfect here. The problem is our own attitude toward it isn't perfect the way in the spiritual world where we existed as Spirit.

Q. How do you stop the Wheel of 84?

A. I believe that it is possible to stop the wheel of 84, or at least attempt to slow down the wheel so we may get-off the wheel (so to speak) and attempt to slow down the rebirth process. I believe that the key elements I can suggest to those who wish to stop the rebirth process earlier to practice the *Stalking the Spirit*— **process**

Q. What is the 'Stalking the Spirit" Process?

A. To be perfectly honest with you, I too, like most people, used to believe that when we die, that's it. One life, one time and then heaven and hell. But, when I see genius and people with disability, I can't help the injustice or unfairness to human kind, or is it un-justice or unfairness? Nobody forced us to be born. We were all given a choice to come into this physical body. We were given the 'will' to come or not to come here on the planet earth. The fact is 80 to 90 percent of all Souls in the Spiritual world don't ever chose to come. They choose not to be born in this physical body or in this physical world *and sacrifice a spiritual world.* They chose **not to enter into a condition called sacrifice.** In the spiritual world where they existed as spirit, as a pure love, and looked down into this material world, and from that high plane of love they saw that perhaps, they couldn't do everything perfectly as in the spiritual world they existed and chose not to take a chance with the good life in the spirit world. They did not want to commit to thousands or rebirth processes to undo what they might do. **It is said, that only the adventurous, more** daring souls in the heaven ever decide to come here on the planet to come.

But, we are not concerned about the souls in heaven who did not come, our concern is with the souls just like us in the physical body right here, right now who want to find a way not to be forced to come back again here on earth once they return home into heaven. To be perfectly honest with you, I too, like most people, did not believe in this 'mumbo-jumbo' about the wheel of 84, or any rebirth or reincarnation and so forth stuff until I learned the *"Stalking the Spirit"* process—**Seeking God 24/7**

My own religion certainly did not believe in these things. I was taught that when we die, that's it. One life, one time and then heaven and hell depending on how you spent the life here on earth. Fear of hell and the rewards of heaven were the themes of most of my religious beliefs. But, when I see genius people on earth and people with disability, I can't help the un-justice and unfairness in human lives.

Perhaps, being born a genius is a reward for having lived many lives rightly, and likewise; disability is the punishment for having lived any life wrongly. Then, suddenly, a third notion comes into my own mind that nobody forced me to be born here on earth. I was certainly given a definite choice to come here on the planet in my physical body. I was given the 'will' to either come or refused to come here on earth at the time and space. In fact, it is estimated, that

80—to 90 percent of all population in heaven don't ever chose to come. They choose not to be born in this physical body or here on earth and sacrifice the spiritual rich, easy living in a spiritual world. Then why should they choose into enter a condition called sacrifice. Perhaps, that's why spiritual masters of all ages often say: *"only, bold and adventurous get to visit the physical world."* In the spirit world where they existed as spirit, as a pure love, and looked down on to the material world, and from the high spiritual planes of love they saw that perhaps it would not be easy to do everything perfectly as in the spiritual world they existed, and the fear of failure and disappointment perhaps, took hold of them and decided not to come into the physical world. I mean, why should they take chances with a good life in the spirit world? Perhaps, they did not want to commit to living the idea of thousands lives.

So—we are not concerned with the souls that exist in the spirit world. We are only concerned about souls who are right here, right now in this physical body in the material world who do not wish to return at the end which is death. They wish to make this life-time the last-time they ever live here on earth in this physical body. And find out who we are, to find out where soul realm is?…………..Can it be done?

Well, I, sure think so. I call it the *"Stalking-the Spirit" process. Here's how I think it can work for all those who are thinking along these lines.* I start the *Stalking the Spirit* by realizing that **I do need to make peace** with everyone in my life. Why? You may ask: My answer: *Everyone lives inside me.* **Just think of it!**

The funny thing is that it doesn't really matter if they are living or dead, or even if I'll never ever see them again. **If they create discord within me, then I have to make peace with them—this is especially true for your parents even if your parents are dead. Who so ever hurt parents, hurts God—for Sure.**

In meditation, I've my intention to stalk the Spirit. I visualize, imagine or pretend that the Spirit then starts to love me, and to be loved in me. I move more and more into the Spirit, and a serenity happens in me. I sense the presence of God. When I experience this serenity it is as if I touch God. I feel and know I am the beloved and I believe that by asking for forgiveness from everyone, and repenting for my wrong doings and consciously admitting them God has forgiven me and there will be no need for me to reborn again in the physical body here on earth because **God has a different task for me in heaven and become a**

Co—creator with God in Heaven. Forgiving myself and asking others for their forgiveness was the hardest.

It is extremely important that you and I do understand that you and I are here and now in the physical body on earth because we did things incorrectly at some time in our existence. We did not do it rightly and we are back. Try to get this one truth right and there will be no need for the re-birth process.

Q. My Soul lives—What's that?

A. My own Soul—like most Souls on earth at this time and space lives in this world, got married, have kids, spend my life in slavery to car payments, house payments, works eight hours a day after day until the end which is death. It is important to understand something: I can take none of that with me.

The only thing that I can take with me, and going to live, and never die—is my soul. If I wish to make this life my last life that I ever live here on earth in a physical body, I must get this intention very clear: ***"God, whatever you want me to do here for you, I'm going to do it."*** My spiritual teacher used to say this in a different way: I'm keeping my eyes on you. Lord—only You."

What that means in plain language is that I'm only doing the things that brings me closer to God regardless of any distractions that may present themselves. Getting my intention clear and anchoring it inside of me is the essence of *Stalking the Spirit.*

For me, it helped me reduce my own life to just one thing: *"Seeking God 24/7."* I consciously show my love for God, who loves me—always.

One day a fellow asked me, "**Is Stalking the Spirit just positive thinking?'** I said, "What do you mean, *just*?" But no, it is not *just* positive thinking. Positive thinking is not the same as critical thinking. If you practice positive thinking, you' feel you've failed when you find yourself, in negative thinking. And this can be very discouraging, especially like me, who used to have a tremendous talent for negative thoughts. My spiritual teacher preferred to called it, **to practice critical thinking**. He didn't mean "critical" in the sense of "criticizing." Critical thinking is the process of examining the possibilities, looking at potential outcomes. It becomes negative only if I project my emotion on it. But, my spiritual teacher said: "If I can employ my intellect, just **observing,** looking, sorting, I can turn the possibilities into usable commodities. I asked the spiritual teacher, "How does it work? He said, "here is a little metaphor. You go into a dark room, looking for something. You're not sure where exactly it is in the room. Rather than groping around in the dark for it, the critical thinker looks first for the light switch. When the room is flooded with light it is an easy matter to find what you are looking for. Since the direction of this critical thinking is positive, yet **it's not positive thinking. What is it? It is positive focus. Why positive focus, rather than positive thinking? With positive thinking, we can be drowning but telling ourselves that things are just great. With positive focus we tell ourselves things will be great—as soon as we get to the shore. Then we focus o the shore and get moving. We say, "I am moving toward a goal. I see it.**

Excerpt from the book: **Spiritual Warrior –John-Roger – D.S.S.**

CHAPTER 8

Critical Thinking as Soul Awareness

My spiritual teacher has taught me that critical thinking is a process of examining the possibilities, looking at possible outcomes. Here are fifteen spiritual exercises that have truly given me more practical experience in Soul Awareness and assisted me in converging my Spirit back into alignment each day. I start this Soul Awareness Journey once a month for fifteen-days. I start each day by reading the designated message for that day. Each day is designed to provide me a focus for my Soul awareness as I move my intention along the message for that day.

Then, at night, just before I go to sleep. I try to re-read the same day's message again and write a short paragraph about my own inner experience. My goal is to change patterns and living in conscious alignment with the Soul. These fifteen spiritual exercises give more peace and centeredness to my own life no matter what challenges I am presented with. These fifteen spiritual exercises are designed to affirm and strengthened **what is best in me**—and avoid the traps the mind lays for me to fall into. I have regularly gone back to these fifteen spiritual exercises to be reminded of what is so easy to forget in the middle of our lives responsibilities and distractions. My spiritual teacher taught me that:

"IF I PRACTICE THE INNER WORKS OF MEDITATION AS OBSERVATION—AND DO REGULAR SPIRITUAL EXERCISES, AND CONTEMPLATE, THEN, ALL THIS WILL GRADUALLY BECOME FAMILIAR AND SECOND NATURE TO ME. - John-Roger—D. S.S.

SPIRITUAL EXERCISE ONE

My spiritual master has taught me that I came into this world for the sole purpose of fulfilling my spiritual promise which is: *to find out who I am, and to find out where the Soul ream is in the hierarchy of the realms of spirit*—and to go there, and have a co-creative consciousness with God. This is my sole purpose on this planet earth. But, my own mind plays devil's advocate in the **left-sided spirit** (Spirit has the Left and Right sides); that is why mind is my enemy and I accept it not as a victim no matter what is happening. I let the right-sided Spirit move me with its knowledge and inner wisdom. Sometimes, it warns me ahead of time, and other times it just walks me into a situation and sees how I handle it. Spirit makes my everyday life magical when I try to open my 'third-eye' and activate the Pineal gland of my brain to experience myself as a Souls and as a one with God not, just in theory but, living reality in my daily life. And, what will be accomplished by visualizing myself as a Soul and as a one with God? You may ask: My answer:

This is my prime directive that I work under. This is where my satisfaction and my fulfillment lies. **This is my spiritual promise.** The purpose of this discussion is not to talk about the separation between the left and right sides, but to bring me to the oneness of the side I am in. Then I will see straddle the line automatically because I will see rightness and its value and the leftness and its value. **The Soul is Both.** I align my Spirit from both sides. When both are balanced there is perfect equilibrium, like a battery, where positive polarity and negative polarity are equalized If you **lean** too much to either side, you will lose that balance. The job of **alignment** with the left and right sides of spirit flows over into EVERYTHING.

SPIRITUAL EXERCISE TWO

My spiritual master says: "It is obvious that the Spirit does not care if it is fair or not fair. Spirit is ruthless in the sense that if my *intention* is not directed toward it, it does not reveal It-self to me. I'll say 'amen' to that and I'll tell you why? I've spent more than thirty-five long years in my spiritual pursuits instead of reacting to the material world. For thirty-five years I have sacrificed anything and everything but, not my God-given power and the privilege to take full and complete possession of my own mind by observing my own mind's thinking 24/17.

Spending thirty-five long years in spiritual pursuits, and sacrificing everything to keep my inner intention 'fixed' only on my prime spiritual goal, is an experience, not calculated to give you a sustained hope, I assure you. But, after thirty-five long years of trials, tribulations, and troubles that I have gone through it, the Spirit, did not even say "hello" to me or do anything, it seems to me, anyway, like a gross unfairness. I often wondered: "What is this thing inside of me that stops me from knowing what's going on for such a long time? What I've found that it was my own mind because my own mind will challenge me to demonstrate just how much I mean in my desire for converging my Spirit back into alignment. This is why I say that the mind is my enemy. Mind will do anything in its power to keep me from knowing what is going on. My mind is often testing, doubting and holding back. But, you know what? My mind all these tricks actually makes me more determined for coming into alignment with the Spirit. **I'll bet that my mind is afraid that I will leave it behind when once I converge with my own Spirit.**

SPIRITUAL EXERCISE THREE

My spiritual master taught me that: "When I was born in this world, I left the spiritual world. In the spiritual world where I existed as Spirit, as pure love, where everything was perfect." So—when I decided to come into this material world, I find that it does not always go as expected the way I saw it when I looked down into this material world and from that high plane of love I saw where I could do everything perfectly. But, in the place I was looking from, everything looked perfect. The spiritual master continued: He said, "So then I decided to go into this place called Earth—and although everything here on earth is still perfect just the way I saw from the high plane of love—I just don't like it the way it is. The problem isn't what is here. The problem is in my own attitude toward what is here?

What I am trying to convey to you, said my spiritual master, that when I existed in the Spirit world, **I existed in the spirit body** and not in the physical body. In the physical word I was born with a physical human body with two eyes and live in the 'duality' of the physical world. So—I see everything here on earth with two aspects, good or bad or real or illusion, happy and unhappy, pain and pleasure and so on. Not until, the spiritual teacher said: I open the 'third-eye' and activate the Pineal gland of my brain can I see everything perfect just the way I looked at the high plane before deciding to come here on earth to fulfill a spiritual promised I made with my creator God. **The sad thing is that by seeing through the two** physical eyes, I see the perception of separation with my creator God because my two eyes 'shut-down' the spiritual 'third-eye'. **My goal is to correct perception.**

SPIRITUAL EXERCISE FOUR

Spiritual masters of all ages who have spent a life-time visiting the realms of Spirit through the 'third-eye' and activating the Pineal gland of brain say that "We don't really belong here on earth—*spiritually* that is. That is why, we have such a hard time making ourselves do what we want to do according to our intention because **our intention only function in the Spirit. Sure, we have advanced enormously** technologically through using mind rightly, but we are still acting like the stone age or during the biblical days by using the mind wrongly. That is why the mind is our biggest enemy because it **will go against the human race in the matters** of Spirit. The mind makes sure that as human being, we never ever find out how to **open the 'third-eye' and activate the Pineal gland of brain to open-up sort of a** passageway to all the mystery of the inner-worlds. Opening the 'third-eye' is about seeing through the eyes of the Soul—said my spiritual teacher. It's about making your everyday life magical by spending more time in spiritual pursuits instead of reacting to the material world. **And, when you really know that you'll live in** freedom and the fulfillment of your spiritual promise. The point I am trying to make here is that only by opening your 'third-eye', the inner-eye, the spiritual-eye as it referred to in the East, can I correct the perception of separation from God. **I do my level best to open my 'third-eye' as often as I can. I can do this anytime,** anywhere, day in and day our seven-day a week, 365 days a year after year until the end which is death. **The key is that we don't belong here—spiritually. "We are engrafted into this body." John-Roger – D.S.S.**

SPIRITUAL EXERCISE FIVE

My spiritual teacher taught me that: "There is no need for me to do what I already know how to do, or try to learn what I already know because I need to learn what I do not know—and what I do not know how to do. The funny thing is that I spent more than thirty-five long years in serious spiritual pursuits not knowing how to open my own 'third-eye' and activate the Pineal gland of my brain. Perhaps, that is why I always remained one step behind my mind in its effort to go against me in my spiritual pursuits. I could never really overcome the five passions of the mind namely: *Anger, Greed, Lust, Vanity and attachment to the material world.* I never did really learn that the Spirit has two distinct aspects—the Left side and the Right side of the Spirit. I didn't comprehend that the mind plays the devil's advocate in **the Left-sided Spirit and the divine love exists in the Right-sided Spirit. The problem is that both, the Left-sided and the Right-sided Spirit are needed for** coming into alignment with the Spirit—God. Most human beings, unconsciously, perhaps, align either with the Lift-sided or the Right-sided Spirit, as a result, the converging with the Spirit, as a whole, or as a one with God never takes places.

The human mind loves it so mind can keep human race attached and spinning into the material word. **The mind knows very well, that once the human race will be** coming into alignment with the Spirit, it will surely leave the mind behind because the, **human will learn to** 'bypass' the mind and **free the Soul** to travel into the positive or higher realms of Spirit above the Soul realm. **Human will leave mind.**

So—said my spiritual teacher, *"your destiny what you are here to learn and what you here to do is—* sitting inside of you. So is the dark side; so is the enemy. How hard, said the spiritual teacher, is it to accept this, that the Light (Spirit) and the dark (mind) can an *must* co-exist within us. In the Christen bible, it is written: *"Seek first the kingdom of Heaven. it does mean learn and to do* In all honesty, I can say this, nothing has influenced my own life in my spiritual pursuits than what I learned from my spiritual teacher about accepting the enemy within and mostly about my coming into align with the Left-sided and the Right-sided Spirit and learning the concept of 'convergence'. In the left and the right sides of Spirit, I **literally found the break down the qualities associated with these sides of the Spirit, the aspects of the Left Side and the Right Side because both sides are** needed and necessary to maintain the balance of Spirit. I visualize or imagine or just pretend that my Left-sided Spirit is dark, while my Right-sided Spirit is Light,

My Left-sided Spirit is a Path away from God, my Right-sided Spirit is a Path toward God. My Left-sided Spirit is Earth—centric, and my Right-sided spirit is Spirit-centric and so on. The very first glimpse of coming into alignment with both sides of the Spirit came as an **act of 'grace'**. This is when my own mind meets my Spirit in 'converging' my Spirit back into alignment. My only regret is that this act **of 'grace'** came into my own life at this late stage in my own life. This act of 'grace came as an awakening process which was the *separation of the thinking of the mind—and my own awareness of the mind's thinking.* For me, it was a proof positive and gave me the legitimacy of the fact that I am not my own mind. I'm a Soul, a divine love. I became aware of myself as a Soul and as one with God—as a daily living reality. I have now reduce my own life to seeking God 24/7.

SPIRITUAL EXERCISE SIX

Spiritual law say: if anything can shake me—*spiritually*, it will most likely be done by me—and my thoughts and feelings. The point is that *I* will shake myself harder than anyone else can shake me. This is why the mind is my enemy because it will go against me in my Spirit and mind will **win**. It seems as if the mind's goal is to destroy my chances of my attempt in converging my Spirit back into alignment.

The funny thing is that for thirty-five years, my mind had a total 'strangle-hold' (so to speak) on my head, never ever assisting me in my spiritual pursuits. Instead my **mind made me reactive to the negativity of people, events, circumstances and situations in such a way that I was always spinning around in the lower and** negative realms of Spirit. My mind made sure that I never know the two aspect of the left Side and the Right side of Spirit, so I completely ignored the Left Side of the SPIRIT, and let the Right Side of spirit dominate my own life. The mind must **have been happy, because I could never consciously open my 'third-eye' and** activate the Pineal gland of my brain thus, there was never a connecting heart with head to initiate the process of becoming aware of myself as a soul and as a one with God not just in theory but a living reality in my daily life. Never did I realize that both the Left Side and the Right Side of Spirit are necessary to maintain the balance of Spirit. **I believe very few people on the planet earth know anything** about the qualities associated with these two sides of the Spirit. **The information that flows may seem rather abstract. It's okay if you don't understand it. Just allow your inner wisdom to absorb it because then, you'll experience the you.**

Excerpt from the book: *Spiritual Warrior* **– by John-Roger, D.S.S**

Aspects of the Left Side and the Right Side

Left Side...*Right Side*

Feminine .... Masculine

Dark... Light

Abstract ....Tangible

Soft ....Hard

Passive..Active

Creative ....Destructive

Emotional.. Intellectual

Intuitive ....Logical

Path away from God ....Path toward God

Remember that both sides are necessary to maintain the balance of Spirit. It is sad that I **wasted thirty-five long**

years of my life in trying to find the 'link' to the Spirit where it never can be found. In fact, I did my level best to subdue and avoid the Left Side of the Spirit. No wonder mind played a devil's advocate and having fun with me playing the part of the Left Side of Spirit. Is there any doubt that why most of us keep living here, and keep living here, and keep living here. At some point we say: "Lord I'm tired, release me, refresh me and at some point in time we surrender control. I know at some point in my own life I did surrender control to what is in control—God. It is said that when the student is read, the teacher appears. My spiritual teacher did appear who taught me the two aspect of Spirit.

SPIRITUAL EXERCISE SEVEN

Spiritual master of all ages who consistently build their spiritual endurance through the inner works of meditation, contemplation, prayers, and spiritual exercise recommend spiritual exercises **(such as these fifteen day spiritual exercises) as the** most direct approach to opening the 'third-eye' and activating the Pineal gland of the brain because once the 'connection' is made into the Soul-energy, we suddenly reach a 'state-of-peace' which allows the Soul-energy to activate, we attune to it, we take hold of it and we start to riding back on this Soul-energy into the center—and get beyond time. I'll say 'amen' to that because when I did make the connection with the Soul-energy and reached the state-of-peace, and activated it, I attuned to it and took hold of it and lo and behold I started to riding back on the Soul-energy that is when I was introduced to the book *Spiritual Warrior* by John Roger D.S.S who introduced me to two aspects of the Left Side and the Right Side of Spirit. **It is said that when the student is ready the teach will appear.**

Please understand what I am telling you may seem rather abstract. It's okay if you don't fully understand it at the moment. It took me forty-five years to be ready to receive it. I am just trying to cut down the time for you to understand it and accept it. The key to remember is this; although both sides of Spirit are necessary to maintain the balance of Spirit; nevertheless, only through the right side of the Spirit can you and I go into the Spirit and have an alignment with it. For me, this is the monumental key in converging my Spirit back into alignment. If I go into the left side of Spirit then, I'll go into consciousness that will pull me down. (Spiritually it's called hell).One thing I've learned from my spiritual teacher is that "people will try to antagonize me, baiting me to strike at them". But, I should do my level best to withhold the strike at them. Why? You may ask. My answer: **"the karma you will set in motion will be worse than any blow."** …. Look at your antagonist and say, "Get behind me. If I strike I fall. Many spiritual teacher offers the other cheek knowing full well that the karma-pattern they set in motion will be worse. The prime way to build endurance—spiritually that is, through adversity. We are strengthened through adversity, and how we handle the adversity is the critical measure of my growth. Anyone can stand and argue and yell back; anyone can call me bad names. But, when someone call me bad names and I do absorb it I gain strength from it. You see the face of the person calling me names when I refused to fight.I've just lost me an adversary. My spiritual teacher used to call people who try to antagonize me, and just waiting for me to strike back at them as the "Petty Tyrant". They bug me with impunity, and often show me where I'm going in relation to my intention. I've noticed that kids, and spouses are often expert in this knowing how to push the 'hot-buttons' just at the right time to antagonize me. The funny thing is that I often thanked them because they can help keep me in line with my intention. I say to myself that I may not have any control over what the Petty Tyrant say, do or even think about me but, I do have a full and complete control over what I do, say or even think. For some reason, most of my adult life, I was always angry, impatience, short tempered, and quick to react and fight back until the nature had enough of my temper and taught me how to be humble. A few years ago, through my own stupidity and mistake, I lost everything that was precious to me; my home, my belongings and my business. Down on my luck and no place to go to, I began to wander around searching for myself and some answer to make my own life bearable. During the day I spent much time in local parks and in public libraries because they were warm and free. Hoping to find the royal road to riches and fortunes, I joined several spiritual mystical and spiritual organizations to help find where I had gone wrong and how I can correct it. But, the truth somehow seemed to be always a step ahead of me. Day by day, I sank deeper and deeper into depression. I began to blame God for all my failure and misfortunes. I was totally broke financially, emotionally and especially spiritually. Then, finally, out of depression, I made some drastic changes; instead of feeling sorry for myself and blaming others for all my own mistakes and stupidity, I decided to meditate every night over a long periods of years. During the day, I began to read every spiritual book that I could lay my hand on. Through the act of 'grace' I was introduced to the book *Think and Grow Rich* by Napleon Hill

He said: *"In every adversity, there is seed of equal opportunity."* He also emphasized the fact that "Every adversity, every failure and every heartache carries with it the seed of an equivalent or greater benefit." My spiritual teacher used to say: "We are strengthened through adversity, and how we handle the adversity is the critical measure of our growth." These were powerful statements of the facts. Fortunately, I decided to handle my adversity through meditation, contemplation and prayers. For me to even think that someday, I will be a motivational speaker, an author a business man was no more possible than going to the moon but, it all happened. My spiritual exercises helped converge my spirit back into alignment.

SPIRITUAL EXERCISE EIGHT

MSIA founder John-Roger, D.S.S. has a message for those who want to help others and be calm by keeping in mind these three things as we go through life, and they are our guidelines. **First,** *Don't hurt yourself and don't hurt others.* **Second,** *Take care of yourself, so you can* **help** *take of others.* **Third, Use everything for your upliftment, growth and learning.** Just so you know, John-Roger is my spiritual teacher. He taught me that "don't get involved in things that are not my immediate level of concern". Why? You may ask? My answer: "Because John-Roger says:

Don't take on someone else's concern. If you take on someone's karma and start to carry it, you both will be responsible for it. Some well meaning friends don't let go and start to carry other's karmic burden. The sad thing about this is you delay them by your supposed idea of friendship. Don't take someone's karma away too soon.

This is really caring for your friends in the greatest way and avoid the suffering all over again through the same karma-pattern. My spiritual teacher said something that I always remember. He said, It is important that you understand something: "You are here on this planet because you did things incorrectly at some times in your existence. **You**

did not do it the way it was to be done and you are back here." And, what's more this may not be the last time if you continue on as you are doing. Do not place value on things in the world, but place value on the things in your Sprit. From out of your Spirit move into the world and let your Spirit direct your motion. Do not let your thoughts, feelings, or ego move you; let your heart move you. It will move you with its wisdom and knowledge.

SPIRITUAL EXERCISE NINE

My spiritual teacher says: "That there are going to be times when I am forced by the situations and circumstances to look more deeply at *who I am* and *what I am about* ". He said to me that during those moments take some time to look within myself, and see *who is in there, and become one with it."* A few years ago, due to a failure in a business venture in the Middle-East, I was forced to look more deeply inside myself at who I am—and what I am about? I began to spent much time in doing meditations, prayers, contemplations and spiritual exercises. Then, in the hour of my deepest meditations, I discovered that inside me, who I am as an eternal being meets, the person who is here temporarily. Here the Spirit, the emanation from God, meets me, the *self* I know. For me this is the point of convergence where my Spirit and I meet. Ever since, this revelation of the concept, my spiritual teacher calls "Convergence" I've become aware of the two aspects of the Left Side and the Right Side of the Spirit. The most amazing thing about this is that when Spirit and mind move to the left, I can be very irritated and yell back. But when they move to the right, I say "Aha!" I see the events of the movement more clearly, and new ideas come forward, often quite rapidly. For example, writing this book intuitively flashed into my mind during one of those: "Aha!" moments. I can assure you that none this manuscript came from my own intellect. Every single word came intuitively from inner guidance through the flashes of thoughts, inspiration and hunches of what to say. You might say that I was just 'ghost—writing' (so to speak) this book by following an eternal being within me.

The funny thing is that when I did find who I am, and what I am about, I found the true me inside me as a spiritual being having a physical experience here on earth living temporarily in this physical body. Amazingly, I found that I really did not care whether I live or die. Death had no threat or fear for me anymore. Death seemed as natural as breathing. And, for some reasons, I began to rehearse death while still living in this body. I wanted to make sure what my last words would be during my last moments here on earth. I began to learn to see death as a release from the pain and suffering on this earth. I began to welcome death as a real friend.

For me, death is transformed from the grim reaper to the giver of new opportunity for a Spiritual life by having a co-creative consciousness with God. I do not care if I die because that part of who I am, inside as an eternal being will always exist, so for me dying become a grace. My spiritual teacher told me that: **The only thing that you and I can take with us—the only thing that is going to live, and never die—is the Soul.** Speaking for myself, since I don't know the moment I am going to die, so I can pray, and forgive myself and ask others to forgive me and have my focus on God *at the moment of death*, I've deliberately *'formed'* a habit of Stalking death by rehearsing my last words: *I did the best I could, God!* I do only that will bring me closer to God regardless of any distractions. Seeking God in every moment of life is called Stalking the Spirit. One easy way for me is to visualize myself moving the Right-Sided Spirit back into alignment with my Soul.

In my own imagination, I can feel the sensation of the bright, beautiful and divine LIGHT traveling from my **heart to my head** and flows out through my forehead.

SPIRITUAL EXERCISE TEN

One thing my spiritual teacher taught me is to stop fearing poverty and find the wealth from the Spirit inside me. He often said: **"Do not place value on things in the world, but place value on the things in your Spirit."** As I go about my daily business, I try to move into the world from out of my Spirit and let my Spirit direct my motion. But, mostly, I do my level best not to let my thought, feelings or ego (especially my ego) move me: instead; **I let me heart move me.** It doesn't mean that I still occasionally lose my head or that I wouldn't rather have peace and tranquility than not coming into alignment with my Spirit. So—I let me heart move me it always moves me with its wisdom and knowledge. Sometimes my heart tells me a little bit ahead of time, and other times, my heart just walks me into a situation and see if I had the brain enough to handle. With Spirit with me, I am not ever given what I cannot handle. I see each adversity, each challenge as an opportunity to test and develop my talents impeccably. The point I am trying to convey here is that I let my heart move me. People of the East, where I come from, **spend a life-time doing spiritual exercises working with the heart charka and connecting heart with head** to open the 'third-eye and activate the Pineal gland of brain. 'Third-eye' is the center of our intuition, inner guidance and all spiritual wisdom. It activates all the psychic senses beyond the physical senses. The key to remember is that we use the 'energy-of the heart' because the heart is the center of **all human gut-feelings and intuition and it's closely connected to the guidance from within. It can receive the Light which is responsible for healing the body.**

SPIRITUAL EXERCISE ELEVEN

As I go about my daily business I habitually watch my "self-talk"—what I tell myself. If negativity surfaces in the *form* of fear, hate, jealousy, superstition, revenge, anger, doubts, I immediately challenge it because I know from experience it cannot harm me. My "self-talk" isn't real. What is real is me and that can never really be threatened or hurt. I tell myself that there is nothing going on that can touch my Spirit. Buildings maybe falling down outside, earthquakes may be shaking the cities outside, but I still say nothing is going on. Why? You may ask.

My answer: It happened to the buildings or cities, not me. So—let's come back to our eleven day mind-challenge which is: *Keep ever watchful. When you are truly alert, truly alive and joyfully awake, negative power cannot trap you. To trap you, it has to find a pattern of negativity in which you are involved, run it out, and lay a trap for you to fall into.* But, if you are in the moment, loving right now, blissfully awake and alert, and you come up to a trap, you will see it, sidestep it, and keep on going. I can tell you one thing for sure. This is an exercise that has given me more practical experience in my attempt to open the 'third-eye' and activate the Pineal gland of brain. The 'third-eye' then direct the heart energy to my forehead, behind the eyebrows and out in the whole universe so the internal becomes the external. The heart-energy begins to heal because heart is the center of this gut feeling and intuition and inner guidance. Be sure to put your intention to the Pineal gland of brain (Third-ye), you imagine it there as tiny red dot, or the black or purple dot, just like your full size eye just inside your head.

SPIRITUAL EXERCISE TWELVE

My spiritual teacher always emphasized the fact that I acknowledge Spirit's presence by allowing *It* into my life 24/7 without restriction or conditions. He said:

Spirit does not care how, where, or when It touches you, because It is not a respecter of persons and It does not care what I think about It. Whether I want the healing now, last week, or a in a month—It moves on Its own time. And, my only job is to be ready to receive of the Spirit at any time and at all times. The funny thing is that I spent half of my life waiting, hoping, wishing that the Spirit would touch me (so to speak). I didn't realize the fact that Spirit isn't the respecter of me and It doesn't care what I thought about it. I finally acknowledge Spirit's presence by allowing it to happen for me instead of making it happen. Spirit does move on Its own and Its own time. The very first glimpse of Spirit touching me happened as a act of 'grace'. I vividly remember as if it was yesterday. I recall that that it was noon time and I was sitting in my car eating my lunch in the company—parking lot where I worked. I was reading a self-help book **The Power of Now** by Eckhart Toole about inner guidance and suddenly the Spirit touched me. The chapter of that particular book was: *An Awakening process.* I experienced the Spirit's presence as an **awareness** of the separation of the mind's thinking and my awareness of my mind's thinking. ***I literally became aware of myself as a Soul and as a one with God, and as a living reality.*** It was as if this **awareness** behind my own mind's thinking was **who I am in Spirit**. I was totally awake, totally alert, not thinking of anything. I felt a non-physical being within me **who loves me.**

SPIRITUAL EXERCISE THIRTEEN

My day thirteen spiritual exercise starts with reminding myself each day one of the amazing spiritual law I've learned from spiritual teacher which is: *If God is truly present in the now (and believe me, He is) what concern do I have for the past or the future? What do I care if I live or die?* The only thing I can take with me—the thing that is going to live, and never die—is my Soul. So—I get this one intention perfectly clear, the spiritual teacher said: *"I'm keeping my intention on You, Lord, only You."* To me, what that means in plain language is that I am doing the things that bring me closer to the Lord regardless of any distractions that may present themselves. Like my spiritual teacher said: "What concern do I have for the past or the future?" Getting my intention clear and anchoring it inside of me is the 'mind-challenge' for the day thirteen. I use awareness, behind the mind's thinking as a tool to keep intention in the present moment. That means the most of the things I tend to focus my energy on is in the past or the future are going to begin to seem meaningless. But, I am not dying right now. Why am I fighting what does not exist right now. What is not happening now? If I am going to die now, I am going to die now, whether or not, I am worrying about it? Worrying—the spiritual teacher said:

is a very hard way to die. One of the most amazing truths I've learned from my spiritual teachers is that our bodies, minds, emotions, unconscious, and soul come together in one place right hear right now right here on earth for our growth and upliftment. We come into this world attempting to fulfill certain qualities within ourselves. We usually go about it in many different ways to find what works for us.

SPIRITUAL EXERCISE FOURTEEN

My spiritual teacher taught me that: **"A great deal of stress that people suffer is the result of not living right now, of being totally occupied with the past or the future. This is the cause of so many troubles.** When I cut my concerns for the *future and the remembrance of the past,, I am right here, right now living in the present moment*. The key to remember is this: When I try to *remember* anything in the past or the future—and when I try to *remember* to be here now—the very act of remembering throws me out of the now. If I stop remembering, or I forget to remember, and just be here now, I can *hold* myself in the now—right here right now! For me, observation is the key to be here in this now. Only, I am, capable of observing the presence of God in the now. The most amazing part of observing is that when I, observe, I suddenly seem to reach a 'state-of-mind' and I am in a state of peace, in which my Soul energy actives. And, when my Soul energy activates, I suddenly attune to it—and I seem to take hold of it and we (Soul energy and me) began to start *riding back* on this Soul energy. When I endeavor to get myself to observe with my mind and my ears for just thirty-minutes, I can start transcending the limits of my own 'identity-structure' of my personality. I always do my level best to start to observe *without* judgment, lo and behold, the spiritual answers. I remain at peace. What I have been seeking arrives naturally! I seem to remain at peace. I know, I can never control God—but I can most certainly align and flow with His will. When I have a clear intention toward a spiritual pursuit and or meditating on that intention, the Spirit and mind will begin to converge.

SPIRITUAL EXERCISE FIFTEEN

I earnestly believe from the bottom of my heart that day fifteen of the spiritual exercise is the apex of this chapter. I say this because it sums up the whole idea of the Critical Thinking as Soul awareness. It certainly, gave me the legitimacy (at least to my own satisfaction) that I am a spiritual being having a physical experience. My spiritual teacher taught me that when I go to see the Soul, I mostly see my thoughts and nothing else. So I say, there is nothing else." If there was, I would be able to see it". **I can't see the Soul existence** because it is wrapped up in me. My Soul is what keeps me alive, not my mind. The mind, as strong as it may sometime seem, is not always to be trusted. The Soul is solid ground. This is why my mind is enemy because it will go against me in my Spirit—and it seems to win.

The division between the Left-Side of the Spirit and the Right-Side of Spirit is extremely critical. This is one reason it took me nearly thirty-five years of spiritual pursuit to learn to recognize the subtle energies emanating from the Left and the Right sides of the Spirit. I had never known about the two aspects of the Left Side and the Right Side of the Spirit. Nobody ever mentioned it to me. I believe not many people even know about it. If they did they would use it. As God is my witness, in the left and the right sides of the

Spirit, I found the known and the unknown (the qualities associated with these two sides of the Spirit) because both sides of the Spirit are extremely needed to maintain awareness. (I'll talk more about this in next chapter). The point I'm trying so hard to make is that only through the right side of the Spirit can I go into **the unknowable where God Is.**

CHAPTER 9

Maintaining Awareness

One of the most amazing secrets I've learned from my spiritual teacher is: ***If I practice the inner work of meditation, contemplation, prayer, and spiritual exercises,*** all this will gradually become familiar and becoming aware of myself as a Soul and a one with God, not in theory but a living reality in my own life become a second nature to me. The secret is: ***"To align myself by training my attention on my Intention; the convergence then will 'shift' in its own time."*** I'm given to understand by my spiritual teacher that if the awareness is not maintained, I will definitely lose alignment, so I will lose my sense of the presence of God. Perhaps, that is why, during my adulthood life, I always felt a yearning inside me, a loneliness even when I was with people; I kind of felt alienated and separated, as if I was not a part of what is going on around me at the moment. I made perfect sense to others, held intelligent conversation with others or while talking within a group.

But, to me as if someone else was talking through me. The whole world seemed an illusion. I thought I was going crazy. So I just kept quiet about my personality.

Once I talked to a psychologist, I was told that I had a problem with the 'identity—structure' of my personality and needed help from a 'head-shrink'(whatever that means). Highly educated or intellectual people may have no clue as to **who we are.**

Recently, I was watching the 'YouTube' video of a spiritual teacher, his first words were, "I *help* people to **expand their consciousness**?" How do you expand it?

Have you ever wondered what happens inside the human mind that suddenly changes ordinary people into extra ordinary spiritual teacher? I believe that the following story explain this mental phenomenon. Mr. Harold Sherman, in his famous book: *"The Power Within You"* tells a story about a man named Mr. M.C Mattern who was at the point of ending his own life because of family and financial hardship. However, 'Spirit' somehow led him to Macy's book department where he purchased a book that inspired him and introduced him to his inner—being—the Soul. There is law, if you want to call it a law that says: *'If something can be shaken, it will be shaken. But that shaking will be done by me and by my thoughts and feelings."* The point is that we will shake ourselves by our own negative thinking harder than anyone else can shake us. **That is why the mind is our enemy**. Mind will attempt to destroy and wreak havoc and vengeance and set loose the dog of war on my neighbor, or my spouse, or kids, or even me. I would like to share with you in my own words the story of Mr. M.C Mattern, this is exactly how I became interested in spirituality due to a failure in a business venture in the Middle-East. Mr. M.C Mattern had come to New York City from his home in Pennsylvania, which he had left because of family and economic troubles. He had hoped to get back on his feet in New York city but things, as they so often do when you are quite upset both mentally and emotionally, had gone from bad to worse. Mr. Mattern finally decided, since he owed several weeks rent, was down to last couple of dollars, and had exhausted his prospects and resources, that the only was out was to commit suicide to end the pain and sufferings of present living.

But, there were several little errands he was intent on doing first before ending his own life and one of them led him through the book department on the ground floor of a Macy's store. As he passed a book table, the title of a book caught his eye and challenged him. Book title was ***Your Keys to Happiness,*** by Harold Sherman. The story goes that on a sudden impulse, Mr. Mattern took up the book and bought it with his last remaining dollars. Returning to his room of his hotel, with the poison he had also purchased to take his life. Mr. Mattern thumbed the book in a defiant mood. The very first passage he came across explained what was happening to him. It read: **"Whether you recognize it or not, you are directly or indirectly responsible for everything that happens to you."** Mr. Mattern, almost threw the book out of the window. He had been blaming his unhappy experiences in life on others, telling himself that circumstances beyond his own control had brought forth these desperate conditions and situations upon himself. The last person he wanted to face was himself. He wanted *least* of all to have to admit that *he* may have been the cause of any of his shortcomings or problems. Mr. Mattern, slowly developed an interest. His immediate thoughts of suicide began to recede into background of his mind. "But, wait a minute." He said to himself. *"What was that something that caused me to be responsible for everything that happened to me.?"* And, "How can I ever pull myself out of the tailspin I am now in." Unconsciously, **his Spirit and mind began to move to the Right Side and began to see the events of the moment more clearly, and new ideas came forward quite rapidly. He began to achieve a heightened state of awareness, of knowing what to do next.**

So—he began to ask his inner-being (Spirit) for help and the door to his new life began to open. The secret to which the book referred to suddenly did jump from the page and stood boldly before him. There it was, in plain black and white: ***"You are directly or indirectly responsible for everything that happens to you."*** But, he thought to himself, "What does that really mean to me in my situation?" And, "How can I ever pull myself out of the tailspin I am in now at the very moment?" He kept on asking these two questions over and over again to himself until it became an obsession. The good news was that by asking these two questions his own thoughts of suicide began to subside in the back of his mind and leave his mind as these negative often do when you maintain awareness and align yourself with Spirit. It seemed as if his Soul had taken hold of his thinking, because Soul is always in favor of, biased in favor of life rather than death. (I'll talk more about this later). The story goes that then, all the incessant, compulsive, negative thinking of the mind began to subsided and eventually left the mind, in a sudden flash of thought from within he began to receive the answer and for the first time in his own life became aware of the spiritual truth that human life is precious and whatever was happening in his own life was, in essence the law of the ***cause and effect, or a 'karma-pattern' he had set-up in his own life.*** That is exactly the book was trying to explain that: "You are either directly or indirectly responsible for everything that happened to you." In the East, from where I come from, this law of cause and effect is referred to as *'karma'*. In the Western world, it is simply referred to the law of action and reaction. This law directs, and dominates our life.

What that means in plain language is that whatever happens in our lives we are indeed directly or indirectly responsible for it because this is one of the laws of nature. For me, it has given me the legitimacy to the re-birth process in human existence. Once my spiritual teacher explained the re-birth process by saying that it is very important that I do understand that: "I am here on this planet because I did something incorrectly at some time in my existence. *I did not do the way it was to be done and I am back here.* And, what's more, this may not be the last time if I continue on as I am doing." To make this long story short, with this insight, the Mr. Mattern was directly or indirectly responsible for all this 'tail spin' he seemed to be in at the moment, he decided to postpone the notion of suicide and his desire for life grew more and more. It's odd, he thought, the way most people go through life and never stop to determine the reason for it. This new insight about the law of the cause and effect, or action and reaction, or as you sow, so shall you reap, had certainly awaken (so to speak) his Soul and especially the law of 'karma', had brought love for life and not hate for life. It is said: *Every adversity, every failure, and every heartache, carries with it a 'seed' of an equivalent or a greater benefit."* This certainly had been a truism in the case of Mr. Mattern. Now, the big question in his mind was that, how can he pull himself out of the tail spin he was in at the moment? The answer came, *"Contemplate."* As M.C Mattern recalls that most of his life he did shy away from anything that smacked the religion, the metaphysical and the occult. The word, "Contemplate", had absolutely no meaning to him, other than the vision of people of the East, with long hair, in meditation.

But, Mr. Mattern was willing to try anything to come out of the tail spin he was in at the moment. So he practiced the inner work of meditation, contemplation, prayer, and spiritual exercises, and lo and behold all this gradually began to assist him in *converging his spirit back into alignment.* Unconsciously, his inner-eye— the 'third-eye opened and began to activate all of his psychic senses, intuition and inner-guidance from within and began to see the world through the 'heart-energy.

He began to see the world as a happy place, and to see others as divine beings and as everything interconnected and found a way to blissful living. Mr. Mattern became highly motivational speaker, sought out by every major spiritual organization and became a highly successful Pastor of a non-denominational, ecumenical church with several thousand members in California. He became a truly a 'do-gooder' of the world. This story really touched my heart. I could really recognize, relate to his story because I too, once had thoughts of suicide due to failure in a business venture in the Middle-East. Then, in the hour of my greatest distress, I found my 'Other-Self'—the "Self" I don't see normally when I stand in front of a mirror. This is the Spirit—the God-Self. I began to intuitively realize that the Spirit—the divine part of me has two sides (or aspects) the Left Side and the Right Side of Spirit. In the Left Side of Spirit mind dwells. Our minds play devil's advocate in the left side of Spirit; that is why our mind is our enemy. In the Right Side of Spirit dwells divine part of **who we are**—God. The soul is in the middle. Soul moves to the left-sided Spirit or to the right-sided Spirit depending upon Whether the Left Side or the Right Side allows to dominate at any given moment.

The division between the two sides of Sides of Sprit is very delicate. It took thirty—five plus years of experience to learn to recognize the subtle energies emanating from the two sides. I deafen myself to the Spirit by the five passions of the mind: a**nger, greed, lust, attachments and vanity.** Being human, I was addictive to these five passions of the mind most of my adult-life. These additions were a way of locking my-self into the left side of consciousness, cutting-off the possibility of movement. Imperfection is part of being human, and I wasn't completely open to the movement of Spirit. But, I placed no judgment and I was determined to step forward into this new inner-knowing of the Left Side and the Right Side of Spirit. Suddenly, I started to change my neurological and physiological patterns to see where the alignment energies are coming in. It was up to me to use them to advance my spiritual intention. Now—the joy of alignment flows over into everything I do, including the most mundane aspects of my day-to-day life. I now realize that it s actually easier to live in alignment through the right side, by loving, caring, and sharing. I automatically touch others. This is not to say that alignment with Spirit is not an ongoing challenge. My own spiritual intention sets the direction, and as long as I am moving in the direction—I am doing the best I can. There is nothing else. Finally, let me say this: this information about the Left Side and the Right Side of Spirit may seem rather abstract. It's okay if you don't fully understand it. Just allow your inner wisdom to absorb it. Keep reflecting on the issues suggested here. Remember this. The division between the two sides of Spirit is so delicate that can take years of experience to recognize it.

CHAPTER 10

Knowing Myself as Soul

The word Soul, in the way I use here throughout in this book refers to my becoming consciously aware of my-self as a Soul and as a one with God not in theory but a living a reality in my own life. My spiritual teacher called it Soul Transcendence.

For me, this glimpse of my own *awareness* of my-self as Soul came as an act of 'grace'. I really experienced this 'awareness' as the separation of the thinking of my mind, and becoming aware of my own mind's thinking. I was totally awake, totally alert, not thinking of anything or asking for anything. My own mind was quiet as if the mind is dead (so to speak) and without any thoughts.

In the East it's called the 'no-mind'. All those who have intuitively experienced this 'state-of-mind' do agree with me that this experience of the *awareness* of something in the mind without any thoughts, is a divine part of who I am—I call this *awareness* within my-self, for lack of proper words—my Soul. This was indeed an awakening process for me that took thirty-five years to manifest through me. I suddenly, realized that Soul is one of the divine part of Spirit. The division between the two sides of Sprit is so delicate, it can take years of experience to learn to recognize the subtle energies emanating from the two sides.

And, many people deafen themselves to Spirit for lack of not awareness and lock themselves into the left side of consciousness, and cutting off the possibility of the movement of Spirit. These energies emanating from the two sides of Spirit do not obey any rules.

It's up to me to use them to advance my spiritual intention. It is important to see where the alignment energies are coming in. Alignment with Spirit is ongoing challenge. My own intention sets my direction, and as long as I am moving in the direction of my intention, I am doing all I need to—just do what I can. One thing I've learned is that when I become *aware* of my-self as a Soul and as a one with God—not in theory but a reality in my daily life then, I become aware of my permanent relationship with God, and how God's love is always in favor of life rather than death. It is said that the greatest quality or attribute of God is *love*.

His divine love for us cures all physical ailments often without our knowledge. ***Knowing my-self as Soul has cured the pain in my back spine and enabled me to avoid major back surgery and loss of left foot.*** A few years ago, through my own stupidity and mistake I hurt my back by lifting a very heavy book shelf by myself.

(We forget that we are not as young as we were used to be 20 years ago). An MRI scan showed a herniated disc in my lower back spine. My neurosurgeon I visited for the treatment of my back pain suggested that the back surgery was urgently needed to cure my severe lower back spine pain.

The surgeon further wrote in his evaluation report that if I did not consider immediate surgery on my left foot at once, and if I waited too long for the operation, I might not regain the use and strength of my left foot. In other words, without the operation I might lose my left foot for good. The thought of losing my left foot for ever surely scared me, to say the least. The neurosurgeon has certainly did a good job of instigating fear of losing my left foot in my mind if I did not act on his diagnoses of operation.

He had caused anxiety, depression, and mostly the emotions of guilt and doubts for not considering the only option for surgery to save my left foot. I'm a border-line diabetic and take my sugar pills twice a day.

Everything is under control but, now with this neurosurgeon's report, I was somewhat confused and I will tell you why? My spiritual teacher has taught me that during my meditation I should withdraw my Intention within and put it on the 'third-eye' to open it and connect it with the Pineal gland of brain to activate it.

Then, visualize that there is a door at the center of your chest and concentrate on it and imagine this door wide opens and the heart opens and suddenly bright, beautiful, divine LIGHT enters the heart through the back SPINE and 'connects' with 'third-eye' in the head and direct it to the forehead (behind the eyebrows) out into the universe and the internal becomes the external.

My spiritual teacher emphasized the fact that the 'third-eye' is truly responsible for many healing processes in my body and the heart actually heals your body. To make the long story short, I began to keep the 'third-eye' open as much as possible 24/7 and I engaged my own 'heart-chakra' and imagined **Connecting heart with body and** see my body through the heart-energy, I saw the body as a perfectly healed body. I visualized my body as already healed and without any pain. Sure enough, lo and behold, my body began to heal as if there no pain. The swelling on my left foot began to recede and I was able to walk normally again without the fear of losing my left foot. On my next visit to the neurosurgeon, I confidently told him that I believe that there was a Higher-power within me that can and did heal my ailment, and at this time I do not want to consider surgery.

The following story shows that God's love for each human being, actually heal the body and it reveals, to my own satisfaction at least, the *love* of life drives each soul. As you read this story, I believe that you'll observe that while you are reading it, you were somehow lifted to a higher sense of mental and spiritual elevation. In all honesty, within this story, I did find the 'secret', knowing myself as a soul and as a one with God not, just in theory but a living reality in my own life. It is called ***Soul Transcendence.*** I'm now going to share a story with you I heard recently.

This story is about a talk Dr. Richard Cabot, the dean of Harvard Medical School had given to the Massachusetts Society (MMS). It seemed that Dr. Cabot had been involved in an autopsy of a man who had been killed instantly in a fatal auto accident. This story validates how the heart-energy works with us.

The man whom Dr. Richard Cabot did the autopsy was a man who, as they often, say, was never sick for a day in his entire life. In fact, he never ever taken a day off from his work for any illness or sickness. Dr. Cabot and his team of medical experts while doing the autopsy on that man discovered, that this man had massive scar tissues within his body. The scar tissues showed that his body had experienced *and did heal itself* from all sorts of health problems, including cancer, and various other illnesses. **The doctor said that at the very moment of his autopsy, this man had four other fatal and other unusual diseases in his body.** And, the man had never been aware of it. Dr. Cabot, in his autopsy report to the MMS, said that; **somehow, something in this man's body system had set-up a sort of a 'defense' against these four fatal and unusual diseases in his body.** As a direct result of this autopsy, Dr. Cabot went on to consider the possibility, every human being has this 'healing' power within. Dr. Cabot decided ultimately to report his conviction to the Massachusetts Medical Society that this inner-wisdom, this Higher-power within all of us is always biased in favor of life over death. He then, went on to admit most of our health problems, difficulties, diseases or ailments that we have throughout our lives, we never know about or even experience in our outer life.

This is, Dr. Cabot said, because of the tremendous, 'healing-power' of this energy which is actively working on our behalf within all of us. (this invisible, inner 'higher-energy' within us the doctor is referring to the Spirit—God).

Dr. Cabot had been shocked, and had undergone a certain amount research as a direct result of this autopsy, and discovered some insights into this invisible, 'higher-energy' within us, and his finding had certainly shocked his colleagues and confidants. Dr. Cabot went on to say that this power-full 'healing-energy' (referring to the Spirit), is ten times as powerful as any medicine available to mankind on Earth. When ask, *"What is this powerful invisible 'higher-energy' within the human body?"* Somewhat hesitant but blushing, Dr. Cabot said: *"It was God's love."* Speaking for myself, let me say this that I acknowledge God's presence by allowing it into my life without restriction or conditions. I believe that Spirit does not care how, where, or when It touches me, because it is not a respecter of persons and It does not care what I think about it. Whether I want the 'healing' now, last week, or in a month—It moves on Its own and on Its own time.

And, my job is to be ready to receive of God's love at any time and at all times. For me, one easy way to be ready to receive of God's love is that I put my Intention on to the 'third-eye' (Pineal gland). I imagine it as a really small dot, a red dot, a black dot, or a purple dot or a blue. I imagine this 'dot' inside my head as a full size eye (just the size of my eye) just inside my head. (we call it the Pineal gland) so that it's easier to kind of let my body know where I am addressing my intention. So, finally, my 'third-eye' area is just behind the eyebrows. I sit-up straight have my feet on the ground and have my spine straightened (its important) for my visualization exercise. I keep my feet on the ground, take a few deep breaths, and just relax.

I imagine that there is door that can center over my chest and opens up and bright, beautiful, divine LIGHT enters through the 'heart-center' and travels, up to spine where it meets tat Pineal gland, where that inner-eye directs that LIGHT through my browser) behind the eyes area) and out into the universe. So—the internal becomes the external. I do this spiritual exercise a couple of times and it take me just two minutes to do it. I do it as often as I can. To repeat it, *My chest is open, my heart is open and the light enters through my heart up through my heart up through my spine, meets the inner-eye and travel through the browse on my forehead behind the eyebrows and out into the universe.* I feel the sensation of the divine LIGHT traveling through my own body. With my eyes closed tight, I look up inside my forehead and see the dot (for me the dot comes in blue color), I suddenly imagine it opens up. When it closes again, I try to open again and again. I feel a little pressure in my head and I know it is beginning to open up for me. I know it is safe and natural to open the 'third-eye' God intends for me to open my 'third-eye". When I do this process through the 'heart-energy' the heart actually heal my body I see the world through my inner-vision. I engage my heart-chakra to connect heart with head. (Incidentally, this was my inspiration for the book title).

In the next chapter I will attempt to sum up everything we have covered so far by telling you a little story that explains how we limit our full potentials through the bondage of our self-imposed limitations. If you are like every human being I know, you are searching for solutions to problems and you can use some help. Like all of us you tried all avenues, sought advice from many people and yet problems remain. Well- we believe in you! I believe you'll find the answers in this book.

CHAPTER 11

A Heart-To—Heart Talk

Let me sum up everything we have covered together so far, by telling you a little story. I'll talk and you will listen. Okay!

A beautiful radiant butterfly floats gently through the trees in a deep, carpeted forest. It lights upon a golden flower. It's wings are softly beating. It lays its eggs upon a leaf. The egg hatches into a tiny and ugly caterpillar.

The caterpillar does not know that it has the 'talent' of becoming a gorgeous butterfly. It makes a strong cocoon. True! The cocoon protects it from the constant struggle with the win and other elements of weather in the forest, but, it also imprisons it.

The caterpillar will never be a butterfly, furthermore; it will never realize its full potential, until it breaks the bonds of its prison. A prison that it has made for himself. Eventually, the caterpillar learns to free itself and becomes the gorgeous butterfly and fly away free in the forest.

You, as the seeker of the truth, have joined a spiritual community of the like-minded people who are also seeking for the truth and who share the same desire for the truth—a divine knowledge to help them in every details of life.

You, as the seeker of the truth have taken a joint step toward freeing yourself (like the caterpillar) and to realize your own full potential (like the butterfly) to break the bonds of our self—imposed limitations, by becoming *aware* **of yourself as a Soul and as a one with God**—not in theory but a living reality in your daily life.

Let me give you a brief preview of what you can expect to gain as you start reading the **Connecting Heart with Head** book.

The first chapter deals with the **Knowledge of the Creation by God.** I believe that anyone who has been is a spiritual path for any length of time knows that the divine creation is split into two parts: the lower and the higher planes. The lower planes are the material, realms of time, matter, space and energy—and the Physical Plane, of course, belongs there. The higher plans, your spiritual goal whether you know it or not, are that beyond time and space: **the true worlds of God.**

I always think of the higher planes as the 'training-ground' for my Soul to experience God Realization right here right now on the physical plane. By reading **"Connecting Heart with Head",** and by opening the 'third-eye' and activating the Pineal gland of the brain will allow you to achieve your spiritual goal while still living in this physical body.

The key to remember is this: **You don't have to die to travel into the higher planes (you will do that anyway when you die) but, you can most definitely visit the higher planes while you are still alive here on earth. Just think of it!**

Spiritual masters of all ages who have spent a life-time in spiritual purists call visiting the higher planes as **Soul Travel**—but, to be honest with you, I felt great desire to learn the Soul Travel for its true purpose: **to reach God-Realization.** I did not understand the term. All I cared about was learning how to move to distant places on earth, flying through time and space like a flash of lightning, and mingling in crowds there in my invisible body. That sort of freedom was very appealing to me. I began to imagine my own physical body as house with many stories or floors. I would visualize the lower planes inside my own body and the higher planes outside of by body. I would also imagine myself **on top of the lower and bottom of the higher planes.** (This is where I met the mystical traveler).

The second chapter is titles **Connecting Heart with Head**—which of course, is **the title of this book**. Nothing has influenced my own life more, than learning to open the 'third-eye' and activate the Pineal gland of brain. My spiritual teacher taught me that **in the Left Side and the Right Sides of Spirit, we find the known and the unknown—but God is in the unknowable, and that both sides are necessary to maintain the balance of Spirit. The key is that only through the right side can you and I go into the unknowable and alignment with it.**

Furthermore; the division between the two sides of Spirit is so delicate, it can take years of experience to learn to recognize the subtle energies emanating from the two sides. The sad thing is many people (Just like me too) deafen themselves to Spirit by not knowing this spiritual truth.

As God is my witness, I spent thirty-five years fighting my mind, reacting to the material world, totally indulging in the five passions of the mind and rejecting mind's incessant, compulsive, useless, un-voluntary, repetitive self-talk and inner—dialogues not knowing that mind was also dwelling in the Left-Side of Spirit and **I needed both sides to become as a Soul** and as a **one with God** not in theory but a living reality. Truly, this is the monumental key to my self-discovery.

My deliberate monitoring of my own thoughts 24/7 for thirty-five years, and taking full and complete possession of my own mind at all times and at all costs is in reality left-sided energy and I was locking myself into the left side of consciousness, and cutting-off the possibility of movement of Spirit. I was totally being judgmental and my mind loved it and played the devil's advocate making sure I'm spinning around in the lower material world and not move into the higher God's world. Once I understood I cannot **have control**, I surrender control to **God.**

The chapter three talks about **Spiritual Beings Having Physical experience.** We are now finding that people, around the world, who are on any spiritual path are very "Spiritual-people"—and yet *not* necessarily religious people." I believe the reason maybe that religion is often traditions and rituals _**we do**_! Spiritual is being something _**we are**_! Spiritual masters of all ages who have spent more in spiritual pursuits, instead of reacting to the material world affirm that we are a: *Spiritual beings having a physical experience here on earth.* What could be simpler.

We are—Spirit, a divine part of God. Once I decided to keep moving to the Right Side of Spirit, I keep moving forward. The funny thing is that when I decided to deliberately monitor my own thoughts 24/7, and catch my thinking in the Left Sided Spirit, and move into the Right-Sided Spirit, **gradually I began to move from what I know into what I don't know—the unknown. And, when the unknown becomes the known, then the unknowable becomes simply unknown. Everything starts to move closer to me. It comes toward me as I go toward it—then, the convergence and alignment meet.**

That is when I say: ***God is unknowable—but I know God.*** The point I am trying to make here is that a spiritual path and a religious path are not the same. You can be a very religious person and not a spiritual person and vice versa.

A religious path is traditions, the rituals, a personal thing. But, spiritual path is something we already are. I believe that no one has the right to force others to change their religious beliefs and vice versa. For me, a spiritual path is just a way for a blissful living. In this book, I teach ***Soul transcendence***—which is becoming aware yourself as a soul and as a one with god in theory—but, a living reality in your own life.

The chapter four is titled: *Accepting Mind as an Enemy.* The key to all this is observing your own thoughts instead of reacting, or fighting them during your meditation. I observe the thoughts that come into my mind.

I notice that the more I observe my own thought in my mind, the more they begin to subside and eventually leave the mind. For me one easy way to open that pineal gland of my brain and activate it **for connecting heart with head** is to sit in an easy chair. I take a few deep breaths, and focus on my own breathing and as I begin to do that I begin to put the awareness more within—as an observer mode rather than an reactive mode.

When I am in that meditation, I just observe the thoughts that come in. I don't judge them as good or bad, happy or unhappy, or resist them. I just continue to observe them. The more I observe them they begin to go away from the mind naturally almost as I am not fighting them. The reason all thoughts begin to go away is because I am not giving them energy. And, as those thoughts begin to go away and then I focus on relaxing my eyes, my face. Then, I close my eyes and I begin to raise my brain waves from the beta level to the alpha level where my own mind is generating mostly more alpha waves, more relaxing waves in the pineal gland of my brain and I am shutting-off my physical eyes, and opening my spiritual-eye (third-eye).

Then, with my own two eyes closed, I begin to focus moving my eyes almost uplook at my forehead behind the eyebrows. I am looking at the imaginary 'third-eye' in the size of my full eye, on my forehead. I see totally darkness there and lo and behold, a tiny purple dot appears and I know the third-eye is in the process of opening and activating the pineal gland in the brain.

The chapter five is: **We Can Only Give What We Have.** Not too long ago, I heard a spiritual master tell an amazing true story that **repetition is indeed the mother of all skills. What that means in plain language is that I can know the Soul through the repetition of my direct experience inside me at which time the information on these pages will move out of the theoretical stage to and become experiential—I guarantee it!**

Yes—repetition is the mother of all skills, I say this because you may have noticed that I have quiet frequently repeated myself throughout this book in an effort to impress upon your mind the key ideas in your mind. So—please remember it's not a typo, or error or some editing mistake or anything else. I believe when you read this amazing story, you, too will agree that why I attempted to repeat myself over and over again—many time, repeating the concept (such as meditation, or Pineal gland of brain) verbatim.

This is an amazing story of a spiritual preacher in the Mid-West who had just delivered a most profound, a most powerful, highly motivational and forceful sermon to his congregation during his Sunday church service. This story proved to me the legitimacy, at least to my own satisfaction, the truth of an old adage: *repletion is the mother of all skills.* I don't remember the exact story, so in this chapter I tell you this preacher's true story in my own words. One Sunday afternoon, this preacher had given a powerful sermon about: the *Higher Consciousness,* "It is, in essence, the preacher said, a way or path to God."

The chapter six is: **God is un-knowable but I Know God.**Here's a direct quote from John-Roger, the founder of the Movement of Inner Spiritual Awareness from his book that inspired the major motion picture, *Spiritual Warrior."* He said: **"The mind stops at the limit of the mind; the emotions stop at the limit of the emotions; the imagination stops at the limit of the imagination. This may seem obvious, but it is amazing how many people think that they can use their emotions to solve mental problems and they can use their minds to find God."**

The spiritual goal of this book is to help you find God, in the way I did. We all have perceived notions of what the Divine will look like. But the reality of God cannot be learned through study. "The only way you can learn God is through direct experience inside of you." Perhaps, that is why my spiritual teacher often said: *"God is unknowable, but I know God."* Out of unknowable alone comes spiritual alignment for all of us on the planet. Our intention is to get in alignment.

For me, it came to me as an act of 'grace' It was an awakening process *not* in knowing but in *awareness*. I came into *awareness* of the unknowable—where God Is. But, how can we become *aware* of it? You may ask: My answer: *By coming into alignment with it.* So—how do we come into alignment? A very good question. My answer: **Only through the right side of the Spirit can we go into the unknowable and have alignment with it.** Did you get it? Think about it!

Seeking God in every moment of my own life is called *stalking the spirit.* **I consciously show love for God, who loves me always. I also stalk death by rehearsing my last words, "I did the best I could, God!" I only do what brings me closer to God regardless of any distractions. It works for me!**

The chapter seven deals with **the frequently asked questions** about the mind relationship. This chapter reveals the means by which the human mind becomes a 'connecting link' between your mind and that energy (power) of the universe that helps us reach our full potentials by utilizing our special and unique talent to serve mankind in some small ways. (I'll talk more about this in details later.) But, for now all you need to know is that the whole universe reveals itself to you when you learn to open your 'third-eye' and activate the Pineal gland by connecting heart with head. I can put my Intention to the 'third-eye' (Pineal gland). I imagine it as a really small dot (or a red dot, or a black dot, or a purple dot). For me, this dot comes in the color blue. I vividly see this dot inside of my head as full size eye (just as the full size of my eye) inside of my head. (we call it the Pineal gland) so that is easier to kind of let my body know, where I am addressing my Intention.

With my eyes closed, I look up inside my forehead, between the eyebrows and see this blue-color dot. I concentrate on this blue-color dot until I see the 'third-eye' in it. Suddenly, the 'third-eye' within the blue-color dot opens up for me. I 'feel' the sensation of bright, beautiful, divine LIGHT traveling through the body. I vividly sense the 'heart-energy' traveling from the heart-chakra, through the SPINE toward inside my head and meets the 'third-eye', which directs the heart-energy to the forehead area behind the eyebrows and outside into the universe. And, the internal becomes external. How long does it take to open the 'third-eye' and activate it? It depends upon you. **If you love and trust in God, than you'll find it an easy skill to learn. Only fear and suspicion will hold you back in spiritual pursuits. Fear of the un-knowable (God) is the enemy of mankind.**

The chapter Eight is titled: **Critical Thinking as Soul Awareness.** The main goal of this important chapter eight is to start a fifteen day **Spiritual Exercises** that gives me more practical experience and assists me in converging the spirit back into alignment. The joy of alignment with both sides of Spirit *flows* over into EVERYTHING I do, including the most mundane aspect of my day-to-day life.

For each day, I write my prime intention at the top of a new page in my daily journal. I start each day by reading the designated passage of that day. Each passage provides a focus for my **awareness** as I move my intention. At the end of that day I reread the same passage again and then write a paragraph or two about my experience. **My experience for** *day one* **is that I came into this world attempting to fulfill certain qualities within me. I'm here to find out who I am, and to find out where my home in Spirit is, and to go there in consciousness, and to have co—creative**

consciousness with God. For *day two*, my experience is Spirit is ruthless, in the sense that if my intention isn't oriented toward it, it does not reveal Itself to me.

For *day three* my experience is that when I was born in this world, I sacrificed a spiritual world, and entered here into a condition called sacrificed. In the spiritual world I existed as spirit, as pure love, and I looked down into the material world, and from that high plane of love, I saw everything perfect. The fact is that every in this world is still perfect, it's just my own **attitude** toward everything isn't perfect because I just don't like the way it is. The problem is with me and not the world.

My experience for *day four* is that I don't belong here—spiritually! That is why I have such a hard time making myself do what I want to do. My experience for *day five* is that I am here in this world to learn how to come into alignment once again with the Spirit. My convergence opens up new perspectives, awareness and insight.

My experience for *day six* is my own thoughts and emotions (mind is both and emotions) will shake me harder toward the Left-sided Spirit than anything else.

That is why my mind is my enemy. Mind will go against me in my spiritual pursuits. My experience for *day seven* is that anyone can stand and argue and yell back but when I absorb it and gain strength from it, I have lost an adversary. My *day eight* experience is that I don't get involved in things that are not my immediate level of concern in order to carry others karma. My *day nine* experience is I don't care whether I live or dies because the that part of my (Soul) will always exist. My *day ten* experience is that I do not place value on things in the world but only on the thighs in my Spirit. My *day eleven* experience is I keep every watchful.

Negative power cannot trap me. To trap me, it has to find a pattern of negativity, and lay a trap for me. My *day twelve* experience is Spirit does not care how, where, or when it touches me. My job is to be ready to receive it.

My *day thirteen* experience is What do I care if I live or die? Worrying about dying is a hard way to die. My day fourteen experience is that a great deal of my stress is a result of not living right now, of being totally occupied with the past or the future. Finally, my day fifteen experience is that I can't see my Soul's existence because it is wrapped up in me. The mind, as strong as it may sometimes seem, is not always to be trusted. The Soul is solid ground. The point I am trying to convey here is that keeping **A Fifteen Day Journal has been a spiritual exercise that gave me more practical experience in maintaining spiritual convergence.** This exercise will assist you too, in converging your spirit back into alignment. **I guarantee it!**

The chapter nine of this book is titles: **Maintaining Awareness.** One of the most amazing secrets I've learned from my spiritual teacher is: *If I practice the inner work of meditation, contemplation, prayer, and spiritual exercises,* all this will gradually become familiar and becoming aware of myself as a Soul and a one with God, not in theory but a living reality in my own life became second nature to me.

The secret is: **"To align myself by training my attention on my Intention; the convergence then will 'shift' in its own time."**

I'm given to understand by my spiritual teacher that if the **awareness** is not maintained, I will definitely lose alignment, so I will lose my sense of the presence of God. Perhaps, that is why, during my adulthood life, I always felt a yearning inside me, a loneliness even when I was with people; I kind of felt alienated and separated, as if I was not a part of what is going on around me at the moment.

I made perfect sense to others, held an intelligent conversation with someone or while talking within a group. But, to me as if someone else was talking through me. The whole world seemed an illusion. I thought I was going crazy. So I just kept quiet about my condition.

When I talked to a psychologist, I was told that I had problem with the 'identity—structure' of my personality and needed help from a 'head-shrink'(whatever that mean). Highly educated or intellectual people may have no clue as to who we are.

Recently, I was watching the 'YouTube' video of a spiritual teacher, his first words were, "I *help* people to **expand their consciousness**?" How do you expand your consciousness? You can't? God is Consciousness—Spirit is consciousness—Soul is consciousness. We can become **aware of consciousness** but, cannot expand it.

The chapter ten is called: **Knowing Myself as Soul.** It opens the door to the temple of wisdom known as Soul. It explains that Soul was sent on Earth to experience the rich living on earth in the physical world and incorporate God-like qualities.

It also share the story of a medical doctor who proves that there is a divine power (wisdom) within us that is in favor of, biased in favor of life rather than death. I feel and I'm sure you concur that this is a remarkable achievement for just one volume book, yet all these benefits are yours when you make a commitment when you take the steps to do the **Fifteen Spiritual Exercises.** I believe that keeping the**fifteen day journal is the apex of this philosophy.** It can be assimilated, understood and applied by first mastering the other seven chapters of the book.

Finally, let me say this: As I go about my daily business, I visualize, or imagine or just pretend that I am a *Spiritual Warrior*, not the kind that hits you on the hand of cuts your arm off and lets you bleed to death, but a spiritual warrior, who cut through the mind's negative, useless, repetitive, involuntary inner-dialogues of the mind that goes on 24/7. I watch my "self-talk"—what I tell myself. I know that mind is my enemy because It does go against my in my Spirit. As a *Spiritual warrior* I deal in experience. When I have experience with God, I do realize that God is existence, I realize that in reality, I don't live God, As much as God live me. **I can be as God-intoxicated as I want to. I align myself by training my attention on my Intention ; the convergence will 'shift' in its own time. But, I do always remember that, I have fallen asleep once, and I do not fool myself—I can fall asleep again. If the awareness is not maintained, I'll lose alignment, so I will lose my sense of the presence of God. When your convergence point shifts, try to hold it to open up new perspectives, awareness and insights.**

CHAPTER 12

Seeing Myself as Soul

In this book I attempt to answer the questions of how to live a rewarding inner spiritual life in today's world of constant change and adversity. I'm a practical man and this is a practical book. My approach is that there is no point in having a philosophy, no matter how beautiful, and poetic that cannot be used every day. *I imagine myself as spiritual warrior as battling the distractions and anxiety of the modern life and ruthlessness as spiritual warrior.* I counter negative habits and destructive relationships by changing patterns and *living in constant alignment with Soul.* For me observation, meditation, **spiritual exercises** and journal of spiritual convergence are some of my 'hands-on' tools for spiritual living. It quite literally changed my life. It taught me how to live from my heart, from my Soul and in a way that is more abundant and joyful than I could ever possible imagine. It's rare that one book is both inspiring and practical. Especially helpful is the

fifteen-day spiritual convergence process for experience and continuous references for conscious living from the Spirit. It gives us common sense tools for maintaining our inner focus in this challenging and sometimes disturbing world.

As human beings, we all share the collective search for meaning and return to living in our true—home, the Soul. This story I am going to share with you in this chapter, quite literally changed my own life. It taught me how to live from the heart and from my Soul. I've endeavored to live life internally without attachment.

Not too long ago, I heard a story on a local radio—KYPA— in Hollywood,California. This radio station I was listening to had, at that time, a very highly motivational speaker who was telling a real-life incident. He spoke about a medical doctor who worked in the hospital's emergency room (ER). This was the place where people were brought in after a fatal auto accident or a major heart attack. All people brought into this particular hospital's emergency ward were usually in severe, critical condition, even to the point of near death experience. I'm sure you probably have seen this on television in some of those hospital emergency-room shows where a person is brought in the operating room. He or she is then, hook-up to some EKG or EGG machine and, with the electrical electrodes, given a quick shock with the hope to retrieving the heart-beat and attempting to pour life into the body again.

On a television show, you see a doctor holding two discs, one in each hand, with wiring hooked-up to an oscilloscope where they could see the heart pulse. Suddenly, the attending physician or doctor hits the two discs—***boom!***— ***boom***— and repeats aloud, one, two, three—***boom!***—again on the still unconscious person's chest, one on each side, and you see the person's body lying on the bed literally jerk up on the bed with each electrical shock as the disc hits the chest of the person. If you have ever seen a medical TV show, then you'll know exactly what I'm talking about.

This is what this medical doctor did for living each and everyday, working in the emergency room, trying to put life back into the human body. Many times, the person would suddenly die, and he would verify their death by seeing a very straight line with a deep beep sound on the oscilloscope screen.

But then, once in a while, this doctor would witness that just a few minutes later, some of the human body would come back to life with no apparent medical or logical reasons or explanations, other than the doctor would notice that there would be a very loud pitch, or a "beep" on the screen of the oscilloscope with a definite pulse in the human body along with electrical peaks on the EKG or EGG machine showing the heart beating normally full speed again. This medical doctor saw this miracle (so to speak) or this medical phenomenon in the operating room over and over again in the emergency ward of the hospital he worked at the moment. At first, he thought, that it was just a coincidence, and all those people who got their heart beats back and became alive again were those people who just happened to be lucky people who apparently, just got a second chance in life and got their life back. But, this 'medical-pattern' happened too often to be just a coincidence. The doctor thought that it was indeed a miracle, to say the least, that the human body was dead for all practical, medical and logical reasons but, the Soul was still alive within the body. The point I'm trying to convey here is that this particular doctor witnessed this miracle or the 'medical-pattern' in the emergency-room of that hospital he worked everyday just too many times to ignore this miracle or natures phenomenon, if you will. He wanted to get some answers to this riddle of life.

Then, one day, this medical doctor started his own private search and investigation, to find some answers to this so-called life's miracle or phenomenon that, apparently, put life back in the human body, before his own eyes. This doctor become obsessed with this so-called miracle.

So—the doctor decided that the best way to find out the truth behind this 'entity' or the 'higher-energy' or Source or the universal-power within all of us that is biased in favor of life, that puts back life into the people he operated on, was to actually personally visit all of them, during his days off from work and during the holidays and weekends to get the answers first hand.

So—he decided to visit all those people he actually operated on in that hospital's emergency room and had died right in front of his own eyes—and did come back to life again. As the story goes, this doctor would visit all those people and ask each and every one of the very same questions: **Tell me, what exactly happened during the time that you were a dead person?** (The answer will surprise you).

No one had every asked this question before, but this medical doctor wanted to know the real answer. He visited as many people as he could find to ask this important question for his own private research, so that his findings could be documented in major medical journals for others to read the facts about what happens when we die? (This is a true 'near-death' experience story).

It is said that during the course of his own personal research and investigations to find the real answers, he visited over fifty people who had apparently died in his own emergency-room and did come back to life again. He asked each of his patience the very same question: **Tell me, what exactly happened during the time you were a dead person?** And, how did you come back to life again? He asked this very same question to each of the fifty people he visited for his private investigation and research.

To his amazement, nearly everyone he visited, and asked the very same questions *gave* him identically the very same answer—verbatim! This is what this medical doctor documented in his report.

In essence, what all these patience said was that: *We literally saw ourselves coming out of our own bodies and suddenly we were in the air above you. We could see that you and your staff trying to start the heart beat.* There was no beep on the EKG or EGG machine just a straight line—indicating we were dead and you all gave up on us and left the operating room. But, surprisingly, this was the beginning of a new phase of life for us.

We all intuitively, became aware of ourselves as Soul—a divine part of Spirit—God. The essence of what we saw was a sense of being a spiritual beings and our inner vision opened up and saw a bright, beautiful, divine LIGHT, showing the worlds upon worlds. A strange joy burst in our Souls.

We heard a voice saying: *"We must now bear the duty of gathering up Souls for return to their true home in Heaven. We must act in loving with all beings, creation, world, and God.* With this short message we were returned into our physical bodies." *The only thing that you can take with you—the only thing that is going to live, and never die—is the Soul."* I imagine, just for a moment, that tomorrow is the last day of my life. What feelings does that thought inspire in my?

One thing is for sure. From this moment on, I'll need to be *aware* of the possibility and the certainty of death, and come to terms with it. This means, that most of the things I tend to focus energy on are going to begin to seem meaningless. As I focus on my death, I begin to focus on my priorities; on what is really important.

There is an old cliché' that asks, "if you had only one day left on earth, how would you want to spend it? Perhaps, it's a silly question, but it's worth spending some time thinking about it.

How I die is so very important because it will be my last thought and my last feeling in this life. How I handle the turmoil of my existence is going to determine my placement in the realms of Spirit when I leave here. So they become very, very important. The life I have been living up to this point on the planet has been a rehearsal for death. So, I have to know how to get away from the body cleanly. I have to know where I am going to place my consciousness. That is why the fifteen day journal is very, very important to my spirituality. The more I dwell upon God and God's love and the extension of that consciousness dwells in me.

When it comes to those last moments before I leave, my thoughts will be on that. **And to that is where I will go**. Most of us are afraid of dying. But when I can contact the Spirit inside of me, I find peace, and death seems as natural as breathing. I look death in the face, and this frees me to focus on life. While death is stalking me, I am stalking Spirit. Seeking God in every moment of life is called stalking the Spirit. I constantly show love for God, who loves me always. I also stalk death by rehearsing my last words: *"I did the best I could, God!" I do only what will bring me closer to God regardless of an distractions.* I've now reduced my own life to just one thing. Seeking God 24/7. I do this through a process I've learned through chapter eight: *Critical Thinking as Soul Awareness.*

Working on the fifteen-day journal has revealed to me the 'secret'—*the importance of coming into alignment.*

I let the Right Side of Spirit move me with its knowledge and wisdom. Sometimes, it warns me ahead of time, and other times it just walks me into a situation and see how I handle it! I've no separation between my mind, body and emotions.

In closing, let me say this that over the past few years, my own work and personality have come under heavy criticism by some people who do not agree with what I was doing. Some people in my monthly group meetings and seminars seemed to be anti-experiment and I have always been pro-experiment, trying new ideas and approaches to any spiritual concepts. For me the best response to all these people has been to live happily and successfully regarding of what has been said or done. I have endeavored to live my life internally, without attachment to the world or to what other people say, do or even think. To sum up this chapter, know this: **We are each an extension of God and, as such, we have certain attributes in common with God. One is the power of creation. Part of our experience on the physical plane is to become a consciously aware and responsible creator, and to create those things that are positive**. The Soul, in Itself, is both positive and negative.

It is complete in its energy pattern. Seeing Myself as Soul, in the way I use the term here simply means bridging the Left and Right Sides of Spirit. If I take the Left Sided Spirit in my one hand, and the Right Sided Spirit in the other, and brought the Spirit together so that they touch, I will still have the Left Side and the Right Side Spirit. But I began to merge them I will have the new Spirit—called –Soul in the middle. This new blend in the middle is the point of convergence. This point of convergence is, for lack of proper words: **Seeing Myself as Soul.** The key to remember is that both sides of Spirit are necessary to maintain balance and seeing myself as Soul. When I am moving in the same direction as Spirit, I am aligned, my convergence point shifts and I am able to hold it by observing it. Keeping death in mind is not being morbid. It's being 'aware' that you do not have time to waste.

"So—be purposeful. Not serious, but with purpose regarding what we are doing here. The religious path is serious, and the spiritual path is sincere—and is filled with joy and laughter –John-Roger D.S.S.

CHAPTER 13

Believing Myself as Soul

My spiritual teacher often taught me that: ***Once we understand that we cannot have control then we can surrender to what is in control, God, and let Him continue to run the universe.*** In the beginning of time, God was in all places in an absolute pure state. And in this purity, it was a void—without specific consciousness. In essence, God did not know Itself, in awareness, in Its greater beingness. So God instituted patterns of creation. It created the universes within which was what appeared to be solid objects (which we call planets) and less solid material (which we call space). All of it is God in Its different manifestations. The very first creation after that was the mountains and the land on Earth. Then came the second creation that were the plants and vegetables. The second creation was superior to the first creation of God in the sense that it could grow and multiply on the land and mountains. The third creation was the animals and they were superior to the second creation of God in the sense they could breathe and reproduce after their own kind. They could care for their offspring. The fourth and the final creation of God, of course; the human beings' they were created superior to all other God's creation on earth because only human being were given the Soul, a spark of God that lives in the human body from birth to te end which is death. The whole purpose of this book is to help me *Believe Myself as Soul.* The point I am trying to convey here is that in essence, a Soul dwelling in this physical body.

God instituted a plan that Soul would know every other Soul through experience. Thus, the Soul, which is more directly the spark of God was evolved and given the opportunity to experience all levels, layers, planes and realm of experience and being. A soul can inhibit any form it wishes. Its job, its reason for being, is to experience all it can on every level it can—thereby growing in *awareness* **of its own divine nature.** The Soul that has experienced all is God—and one with God.

My spiritual teacher called it: *Soul Transcendence* which is becoming aware of yourself as Soul, and as a one with God. This experiencing of God is incomprehensibly large and complex, to say the least, so the Soul spends tremendous time in evolving through the realms of experience back into the **awareness** and knowledge of its divine nature. Not only can the Soul, through the human form, experience all the negative realms, but it also can directly experience the positive realms that exist beyond the negative. These realms of pure Spirit really defy explanation in physical vocabulary; they must be experienced to be known. There is no word—it can only be said that they do exist and that it is everyone's potential and everyone's heritage to— someday know of them in direct, conscious experience. The whole purpose of this book is to help you **believe** that you are in essence a Soul dwelling in this earthly body. For this idea to become a part of my own consciousness, I had to be willing to suspend the beliefs that I had growing up. Once I did suspend the old beliefs I used to have, I found that, totally spontaneously, something happened within my awareness. I did not know yet what happened, but occurred to lift me above myself and brought me closer to God.

This was truly a "wake-up" call for me. I remember I called it—***Waking Myself UP.*** Waking up means observing myself to find out what I am doing? This is really an easiest process in the world. It is learning the art of ***meditation as observation.*** I do not judge the mind or the emotions. I *'observe'* them, and the o*bserving* itself dissolve <u>our negative emotions.</u> ***What will be left when all negative emotions are dissolve?*** You may ask: My answer, I'll be losing all negative thoughts. But, if I can observe what is happening and record it accurately, and then place the love in it, that love will move the disturbance. That is how I get free; that is how I dissolve negative thoughts. This process of *meditation as observation*, totally spontaneously, lifts me above myself and bring me closer to God. And, that is how to make it happen every time I **'meditate as observation— to be as deep, as ecstatic, as God-intoxicated as I want to be.'** Observation is a state of detachment, which lifts my into a greater awareness. I become more and more free. My spiritual teacher calls observation the key to letting go. "When something disturbing shows up", he said: and we *observe* it without reacting emotionally, we do not get thrown off balance." Only human beings are capable of observing the presence of God in all things, including themselves. Human beings are sacred for that reason. If only we could understand that simple fact, you would never need to read another self-help book. Believing Myself as Soul, in the way I use refers to waking myself up, which simply means observing myself to 'find-out' what I am doing. Then, suddenly, I reach a 'state-of-peace' which allows the Soul to activate, I attune to, I take hold of it to start riding back on this soul energy.

Mellon-Thomas Benedict's
Near Death Experience—

www.mellon-thomas.com.

"In 1982 I died from terminal cancer. The condition I had was inoperable, and any kind of chemotherapy they would give me would just have made me more vegetable. I was given six to eight months to live. I had been an information freak and I had become increasingly despondent over the nuclear crisis, the ecology crisis, and so forth. So, since I did not have a spiritual basis, I began to believe that nature had made a mistake. And that we were probably a cancerous organism on the planet. I saw no way that we could get out from all the problems we had created for ourselves and the planet. I perceived all humans as cancer, and that is what I got. That is what killed me. Be careful what your world view is. It can feed back on you, especially if it is a negative world view. I had a seriously negative one. That is led me into death. I tries all sorts of alternative healing methods, but nothing helped. So I determined that this was really between me and God. I had never really faced God before, or even dealt with God. I was not into any spirituality and alternative healing. I set out to do all the reading I could and bone up on the subject, because I did not want to be surprises on the other side. So, I started reading on various religions and philosophies. They were all very interesting, and gave hope that there was something on the other side. I remember waking up one morning about 4:30 a.m. and I just knew that this was it. This was the day that I was going to die. I woke up my hospice caretaker and told her. I had a private agreement with her that she would leave my dead body alone for six hours, since I had read that all kind of interesting things happen when you die.

I went back to sleep. The next thing I remember is the beginning of the near-death experience. Suddenly, I was fully aware and I was standing up, but my body was in bed. There was darkness around me. Being out of my body was even more vivid than ordinary experience. I could see around the house. I could see under the house. ***There was this light shining. I turned toward the LIGHT. The Light was very similar to what many other people describe in their near-death experiences.***

It was so magnificent. It is tangle, you can feel it. It is alluring; you want to go to it like you would want to go to your ideal mother's or father's arm. As I began to move toward the Light, I knew intuitively that if I went to the Light, I would be dead. So—as I was moving toward the Light I said: ***Please wait a minute, just hold on a second here. I want to think about this; I would like to talk to you*** *before I go. To my surprise, the entire experience halted at the moment. You are indeed in control of your near-death experience. My request was honored and I had some conversation with the Light.* Speaking for myself, as I read this man's story, I began to indulge myself, in my own imagination, and recall the story of the medical doctor who worked in the emergency ward of the hospital where he witnessed the near-death experiences of people who were brought to the hospital 'emergency-room' after the fatal heart attack or an auto accident. For one thing, it gave me the legitimacy to the Mellon-Thomas Benedict's near-death story. I found that, totally spontaneously, something happened. I did not know yet what happened, but something occurred to lift me above myself and closer to God. I began to meditate— to be as deep, as ecstatic, as God-intoxicated as I wanted to be.

Suddenly, I reached a 'state-of-peace' which allowed my Soul energy to activate. When it activated, I attuned to it. I took hold of it—and I started riding back on this.

Soul-energy into my own heart and through the spine meets my 'third-eye' in my head and the 'third-eye' directs this heart-energy to the forehead (behind my eyebrows) and outside into the universe. So—Connecting Heart with Head

the internal becomes the external. So—let's continue with our story of this man.

As I was saying before: Mellon-Thomas's near-death experience was halted and his request to talk to God was honored and he had some conversation with God.

Here's what happened I share it in his own words: *"I asked the Light, "What is going on here? Please, Light, clarify yourself to me. I really want to know the reality of the situation."* The Light responded. *"Your **beliefs** shape the kind of feedback you are getting from the Light!"* As the Light revealed Itself to me, I became aware that what I was really seeing was our High-Self matrix. Finally, As I returned to the life, It never crossed my mind, nor was I told, that I would return to the same body. It just did not matter. I had complete trust in the Light and the life process. I was given a lesson on how individual identity and consciousness evolve.

I was so surprised when I opened my eyes, I do not know why, because I understood it, but it was still such a surprise to be back in this body, back in my own room with someone looking over me crying her eyes out. It was my hospice caretaker. It was not just a 'near-death' experience. I literally, experienced death.

Itself for an hour and a half. Within three days, I was feeling normal again, clearer, yet different thanI had ever felt in my life. My memory of the journey came back later. **The only thing that you can take with you and never die —is the Soul.**

The body is the most magnificent Light-being there is. The body is a universe of incredible Light. What I present outwardly is not my true self. You see me by reflected Light. But, I am light, *not reflected light. So are you.* Spirit is not pushing us to dissolve this body. Spirit is always in favor of, biased in favor of life rather than death. All the ailments, sickness, and diseases we have in our bodies we never even know off, because Spirit heals all without our knowledge or consent, or demands. The mind is like a six years old spoiled and stubborn child running around the universe, demanding this and thinking it created the world. So I never take people at face value, but I accept people both in their essence and in the way they present themselves to me. *I can face an enemy inside and say. "I love you?'Especially a stubborn enemy inside me? Yes, I can, and I will tell you what happens when I do. Once I truly embrace the darn side (the enemy inside), it turns to help me. Then, I don't have stubbornness, I have determination. The darkness (enemy inside) transformed the moment I accepted it, and the power that was blocking it before now becomes the power of ascension, of uplifting*

We have to go into the dark part of ourselves and love that dark part. We have to acknowledge that the dark side is the part of us. It is in essence, the Left Side of the Spirit. Once I love the enemy inside, once I embrace it, that enemy will transform and yield its power to me. At that moment, I am sitting on the most wonderful wealth of my existence. The ability to do, the strength to do it, and the energy to complete it; that is the true wealth. **Out of that comes our health and our happiness.** This becomes self-evidence to us by **connecting heart with head.**

CHAPTER 14

One Last Secret

I've deliberately kept hidden one last secret from you because the information I share here may seem somewhat abstract. If you don't fully understand it at your first reading, that's Okay; it took me more than thirty-five years to receive it, and then reflect on this one last secret—and it took me another few more years to validate the principles of the process. This book is my attempt to share with you what I've learned and to teach you how you can apply these principles in your own life, whatever your circumstances may be, I know they work because I have tried and tested all these principles time and time again in my own life. As you read it, I urge you to use what works for you and let go of what doesn't. In fact, I've applied that principle to my entire life. I've now reduced my own life to just one thing: *seeking God 24/7.* I do this through a process I learned from my spiritual teacher who revealed me this one last secret which is—*the importance of coming into alignment with the Left Side and the Right Side of Spirit. My spiritual teacher taught me that inside us who we are as an eternal being meets the person who is here temporarily. Here the Spirit, the emanations from God meets us, the self we know. This is our point of convergence: a point of concentration or attention.*

When we move toward the convergence point, we can spend more of our time in spiritual pursuit instead of just reacting to the material world. Surrendering control means we can never control God, so why not surrender control to God!

The division between the Left Sis and the Right Side of Spirit is so delicate, that it can take years of experience to learn to recognize the subtle energies emanating from the two sides. The funny thing is that for thirty-five years, I was completely unaware of the two aspects of Spirit. So, I did my level best to deafen myself to the Left-Sided Spirit and spend more of my time in the Right- Sided Spirit and I was never ever able to move toward the convergence point and couldn't understand why, all my self-control, positive attitude, and taking full and complete possession of my own mind by controlling my thinking 24/7 for thirty-five plus years did not assist me in converging my spirit back into alignment? I spent most of my time in spiritual pursuits instead of reacting to the material world.

Left-Sided Spirit and spend more of my time in the Right-Sided Spirit and I was never ever able to move toward the convergence point and couldn't understand why, all my self-control, positive attitude, and taking full and complete possession of my own mind by controlling my thinking 24/7 for thirty-five plus years did not assist me in converging my spirit back into alignment? I spent most of my time in spiritual pursuits instead of reacting to the material world. I always did my level best to try to get away from people I really didn't like, people who push my buttons and make me uncomfortable, or hurt my feelings. I used positive affirmations and inspirational self-suggestions to squeeze-out the negative thinking of my mind 24/7, seven days a week, 365 days a year after year for thirty-five plus years— and ***nothing really seemed to work.*** It seemed as if all those "petty tyrants" people always won—and I was back in square one (so to speak). Then, once I fully understood this last secret, it hit me like a jolt of lightening. ***Wham!*** It suddenly dawned on me that our minds play devil's advocate in the Left Side of Spirit; that's why the mind is my enemy. And, my mind will go against me in my Spirit.

Although, my Spirit, the Soul is a divine park of God— nevertheless; mind will attempt to destroy and wreak havoc and vengeance and start a war against me. So—the one last secret I discovered is that the human mind is the "petty tyrant".

What I have found is that the purpose of the mind (as a petty-tyrant) is really expose my sense of self-importance, and want to help others; I must not get involved in things that are not my immediate level of concern. I must not ever take on someone else's concerns. For many years, I had this habit of being a 'do—gooder' of the world and helping everyone in everything and getting involved in things that are not my immediate level of concern. Unconsciously, what I was doing was taking on someone's karma and I started to carry it. But, the funny thing is that by getting involved in things that were not my immediate level of concern, the person who originally had the karma still had to carry the burden. So now there were two of us carrying the same karma because this was a karmic burden that is their. I delayed them by my supposed idea of friendship. When I took away others karma burden too soon, I was damming them to suffering all over again through the same 'karma pattern". That is when I began to realize why I was having backaches and headaches and leg aches, it was because I was in something that is not mine. I got out of it. So, in a way, mind is ruthless. Not the kind of ruthlessness that hits you on the head or cuts your arm off and lets you bleed to death, but ruthless in the sense that if my intention is not oriented toward it, becomes the "petty-tyrant". On the other hand, if I let my Left Sided Spirit and the Right Sided.

Spirit work together, I start to change the neurological and physiological patterns and see where the alignment energies are coming from. Alignment with Spirit involves detachment from the world, but it does not mean hatred of the world. *The joy of alignment flows over into everything I do including the most mundane work.*

How few people realize this last secret. It's amazing to know that it is actually easier to live in 'alignment' through the right side, by loving, caring, and sharing I automatically touch others. I don't have to search them out. It just takes place for me. Please don't get me wrong. This is not to say that alignment with Spirit is not an ongoing challenge. I align my Spirit from both sides When both are balanced there is perfect equilibrium, like a battery, where positive polarity and the negative polarity are equalized. If I lean too much to either side, I lose that balance. I pray from the center of Spirit. I let the right side of the spirit move me with the knowledge and inner wisdom. Sometimes, it warns me ahead of time, and other times it just walks me into a situation and see how I handle it. I often wonder how many of my needs are automatically met just when I need them It is a tremendous thing for me to have no separation between my mind, my body and Soul. This way, there is only one Spirit coming into alignment with God In closing: Align yourself by training your attention on your intention: the convergence will shift in its own time. But, I always remember, I have fallen sleep once, I do not fool myself—I can fall sleep again. I know that if I do not maintain awareness, I will lose alignment and so I will lose my own sense of the presence of God. I will feel a yearning inside me, a loneliness even when I am with people; I will feel alienated and separated, as if I am not a part of what is going on. But, by knowing this one last secret, I cannot be permanently alienated and separated from what dwells within me. *I mediate daily as observation.* I engage the heart chakra by Connecting **Heart with Head**. I let the Heart-energy heal all physical ailments and love God!

CHAPTER 15

Pituitary gland of Brain

Recently, I did a Google search to find out what the word Pituitary gland of the brain means? I was amazed to find out more than 40,000 hits showed up on that particular Google search I was doing. And, here is what I found; *"A Pituitary gland of brain is a pea-size body attached to the base of the brain."* Spiritual masters of all ages who have spent an entire life-time in spiritual pursuits instead of reacting to the material world **affirm** without any room for doubt, that for visualization purposes, these spiritual masters visualize, or imagine or just pretend seeing this Pituitary gland in the brain *as a tiny 'dot' in the color or red, or black, or blue or in the color purple (my favorite dot),* in the size of the full eye, in the back of the head—and—this is important, **connected** to my heart. One thing my spiritual my spiritual teacher has taught me is to do **Meditation as Observation**. I have done meditation for thirty-five plus years and all I could see was a 'dot' or nothing—I mean—complete **darkness** in my forehead. I used to get irritated and angry. But, my spiritual teacher used to say: ***Remember, I don't have to 'do' anything with that darkness. Just get rid of your false expectations of what spiritual experiences mean:* JUST BE SILENT AND OBSERVE YOUR DARKNESS because God is speaking through the darkness I see that I.** When I am being so uptight and resenting it I fail to hear God's voice through the Darkness' Each 'dot' of color I see is truly a sign of my Spirit back into alignment.

My spiritual teacher said: ***"If I could do Meditation as Observation***—and place love into, that love will move the irritation and anger—and get free; that is how I can dissolve negative karma. Then, as God is my witness; suddenly, totally spontaneously something happened within me. I did not know yet that happened, but something occurred to lift me above myself and brought me closer to God. Frankly; it was a 'state-of-mind' that allowed me to do meditation as observation and ***make it happen every time I mediate—to be as deep, as ecstatic, as God—intoxicated as I want to be.*** The secret to which I refer has been mentioned no fewer than a hundred time throughout this book. It has not been directly named, for it seemed to work more successfully when, it is merely uncovered and left in sight, where those who are ready, and searching for it, may pick it up. That is why my spiritual teacher tossed it to me so quietly, without giving me its specific name. I must admit, that it took me more than thirty-five years to be ready, and I was searching for it. It became quite obvious to me that the Spirit does not care if it is fair or not. Spirit is ruthless, not in the bad sense, but ruthless in the sense that if My intention is not oriented toward it, it does not *reveal* Itself to me, But, it is somewhat unfair that the Spirit is ruthless, in the sense after all the thirty-five years plus of trials, tribulations, and troubles that had gone through to reach the Spirit by converging my Spirit back into alignment, the Spirit didn't even say "hello—Mushtaq" or do anything—it seems to me like a gross unfairness. (Do you agree?).I often wonder, that what is this thing inside of all of us that stops usknowing what is going on. (Do you know what it is?) Please tell me so I can know it too.

The peculiar thing about the one last secret I talked about in Chapter Fourteen is that those who once acquire it and use it, find themselves literally swept on to success. Here is the bottom line, if you are ready to put it to use, you will recognize this one last secret at least once in every chapter. I wish I might feel privileged to tell you how you'll know if your are ready, but that would deprived you of much of the benefits you'll receive when you make the discovery in your own way. The funny thing about the one last secret is that it has been mentioned no fewer than a hundred times in throughout the book. It has not been directly names, for it seems to work more successfully if it is merely uncovered and left in sight, where those and searching for it, may pick it up. Perhaps, that is why my spiritual teacher tossed it (so to speak) to me very quietly, without giving hints or clues, or giving its specific name to find out if I had the brain enough to understand the full significance of the one last secret. But, in all honesty, let me be perfectly honest with you and tell you that there is no such thing as something for nothing! The one last secret to which I refer cannot b e had without a price, although the price is far less than its value, *It cannot be had at any price by those who are not intentionally searching for it. It cannot be given away, it cannot be purchased for money, for the reason that it comes in two parts.* **One part is already in possession of those who are ready for it.** I've endeavored to live my life i*nternally*, without attachment to the world. If you are ready to put the two parts of the secret to use, then, you already possess one half of the it; therefore; you will readily recognize the other half the moment it reaches your own mind. Guaranteed!

The key to remember is this: *Opening the 'third-eye' and activating the Pituitary gland of the brain has ultimately assisted me in converging my own Spirit back into alignment.* In every chapter of this unique, and one of a book, mentioned has been made of this one last secret which has made *connecting heart with head* possible for hundreds of exceedingly spiritual men and woman whom I've carefully analyzed over a long periods of years. This one last secret was brought to my attention by John-Roger, the founder of the *Movement of Spiritual Inner Awareness (MSIA).* I was so intrigued by the legitimacy of the MSIA teachings that I decided to devote my entire life to the study of the MSIA teachings. One reason I'm so passionate in MSIA teachings is that it is built on the foundation of 'Service and Loving' I sometimes visualize, or imagine or just pretend that MSIA was made just for me—because, it is so compatible how I am inside and how Spirit works through me. It's amazing how much MSIA teachings coincides with what I've experienced within me as a Soul and as a one with God not just in theory but a living reality in my daily life. You might say that I'm a living proof of the validity of what John-Roger teaches us through MSIA books, DVD and CD's. Please log on: www.msia.org. for more details. MSIA offers *A Course in SoulTranscendence* which is becoming aware of yourself as a Soul and as a one with God not in theory but a living reality in life. **Soul Awareness Discourses (SAD) are for people like you and I, who want consistent, time-proven, workable approach to our spiritual unfolding.** A set of MSIA Soul Awareness

Discourses(SAD) consists of twelve booklets, one to study and contemplate for each month.

As you read each MSIA monthly discourse, you can achieve an awareness of your Divine essence and deepen your relationship with God. (All this has been true for me). Spiritual in essence, MSIA Soul Awareness Discourses (SAD) are compatible with religious beliefs you might hold. In fact, we are finding that people coming to MSIA teachings—around the world—are VERY spiritual people and *yet not necessarily religious people.* I believe that one reason for that is that religion is tradition and rituals—*we do!* Spiritual is something *we are!* Get the picture? My spiritual teacher taught me that: *We are a Spiritual (not physical) beings having a physical experience here on earth.* What that means in plain language is that: *We are SPIRIT—a divine part of God.* The first year's MSIA Discourses address topics ranging from creating success in the world to working hand-in-hand with Spirit. For more information on the MSIA *A Course in Soul Transcendence*—**Please call toll free 1-800-899-2665 or visit the online store at www.msia.org.**

It was my good fortune that Dr. Paul Kaye, a part of the MSIA Presidency in Los Angeles California, encouraged me to train for becoming the *MSIA Seminar Leader,* hosting the Soul Awareness Seminars (SAS) in my own local community to teach people in regard to Soul Transcendence which is becoming aware of yourself as a Soul and as a one with God not in theory but a living reality in life.

(The key word here is becoming aware—*not in theory*). Dr. Kaye took John- Roger's lectures and skillfully recognized the book *Spiritual Warrior—The Art of Spiritual Living.* This world famous book also inspired the major motion picture *Spiritual Warrior.* This motion picture shared the MSIA teachings, and insights.

The funny thing is that for thirty-five plus years, I've literally living the *Spiritual Warrior* life-style. *Spiritual Warrior*— the sound of that **title** was like music, exciting a spirit of love and adventure unlike anything I had ever felt before, surpassing even my first encounter with MSIA teachings. For the first time, I felt like a part of something bigger and more grand. For me this book, in my mind anyway, was a god-send. For one thing, this book gave me a legitimacy to the MSIA and **SOUL TRANSCENDENCE—as taught in the book *Spiritual Warrior.*** I have regularly gone back to this book to be reminded of what is so easy to forget in the middle of my own life's responsibilities and distractions. This book, made it much easier for me to let go **my fears and not to sacrifice** my personal truth just to go along with others. As God is my witness, most of my own adult life, I've always sensed as if a part of me was non-physical (spiritual) and longs to communicate with me but, I didn't understand it. I thought I was going crazy. I remember that once I told about my mental condition to the President of my graduate study college **Columbia College** in Los Angeles, California. He said that I needed to see a 'head-shrink' (whatever that means) You can tell how much the most educated and the most intelligent people know about spirituality. He had no clue as to what in the heck I was talking about. The funny thing is that he was the head of one of the largest professional and vocational graduate study colleges in California. He was highly intelligent, intellectual, educated (book knowledge wise) but, *spiritually*—he had no clue what-so-ever as to *who we are* or even *what our purpose in life is.* He was indeed a man of the world—but not a man of Spirit!

It wasn't until I became a full time student of the *Movement of Spiritual Inner Awareness (*MSIA) teachings and started a course in Soul Transcendence—that I began to learn that beyond my mind, body and emotions, there is a Soul. John- Roger, DSS taught me: "**All that you want to be, you already are.** *All you have to do is move your awareness there and recognize the divinity of* **your own Soul." I** earnestly believe from the bottom of my heart that this is what, through the chain of events inspired me to train for becoming the MSIA Soul Awareness Seminar Leader. In all honesty, for me, to even, think that someday I will be the host of the MSIA Soul Awareness Seminars in my local community was no more possible than my going to the moon, because English is my second language and being shy and lacked self-confidence. John-Roger, through these MSIA Soul Awareness Seminars created this opportunity for me to share our gifts, talents and abilities with each others to activate an awareness of my divine essence of who I am and deepen my relationship with my creator—God. In the next chapter I will share a special and unique talent we all have as a gift from our creator—God. I will share how I pulled myself in the 'tail-spin' I was in due to failure in a business venture in the Middle-East. Somewhere, as you read, my true story, it will surely assist you in converging your Spirit back into alignment and will begin move to a higher level of awareness—from the **un-known to the un-knowable—where God Is. This awareness of yourself as Soul will jump up from the page and stand boldly before you, if you are ready for it! When it appears itself, turn down a glass, for that occasion will mark the most important turning-point of your own life.**

CHAPTER 16

A Special and Unique Talent

First of all, let me tell you that I am in no way more special, more gifted, or more talented or even spiritual than you are. I am just like you and any others reader of this book. I am on my own spiritual path and for over thirty-five years I did study with a whole lot of wonderful people, with spiritual teachers, and for me it's a spiritual journey and I am happy to teach you everything I know. Over the past thirty-five years, I've sensed as if my whole life has been a long road to a spiritual path in a series of turning points. Often, I felt as if, I seemed to be going in a direction I don't want to go—*spiritually!* I challenge you to look back sometimes and retrace some early turning points in your own life and, you too, like me, will discover it is absolutely true for you. The peculiar thing about all this is that these turning points in our lives are important, for each occurs at a crucial moment — and are an eloquent tribute to the hand of God in our life. So look back sometimes.

You, too, will notice that at any given points in your life, an invisible force, or Higher Power (call it whatever you want) took control of events and by some miracle sent you more in the direction of own life's purpose in order to fulfill your spiritual promise. You and I, and everyone here on earth, has come into this world attempting to fulfill that promise. When we were born in this world we sacrificed a spiritual world. The problem is not what is here. The problem is our own attitude toward it. We don't belong here spiritually, because our intention works in Spirit.

> There are two things that I want you to know about
> yourself. If you understand these two things and
> take them to your own *heart*, your own life will
> never be the same and you'll will find an easy way
> make everyday life magical. I guarantee it!

First, **you <u>have</u> a special and unique 'talent' to give to others. Now—please** understand that I'm not saying this to you to praise or to glorify you in any way or shape or form (unless, of course, it happens to be true in your own case). I know I had very hard time accepting this truth that *I have a special and unique talent* to give to others. I remember I kept saying to myself, Yeah—sure. **"I've a special and unique talent to give to others."** I almost threw the book out of the window, and I will tell you why? "I was just a foreign student from a country called (Pakistan) and I could not speak much English language, and had very hard time getting admission in some of the reputable colleges and universities in the United States of America. As I've said it before and I think it's worth repeating again because *repetition is the mother of all skills.* It is the God's truth that: *"If some had told me that someday I, would be a motivational and inspirational speaker, and would write a full length book about some of the most intensely complicated metaphysical (*referring to the Pineal gland of brain) *subjects, I would have thought it no more possible than going to the moon with those highly scientists and qualified astronauts in the outer-space" Just think of it!* But, perhaps the biggest proof positive of the validity of my special and unique talent came that for twenty-plus years, I made good living by giving lectures and seminars worldwide professional and financial organizations about principles that can change destiny.

Please understand that I don't tell you all this to brag about me or to glorify myself in any way, shape or form. Far from it. I tell you all this because when you make a habit of becoming aware of yourself as a Soul and as a one with God, not in theory but a living reality in your own life, the whole universe conspire to work on your behalf. Life begins to lead you toward everything you need to make your life purpose a reality. People, events. circumstances, situations just seem to come your way from nowhere. You begin to wonder where they have been hiding during all those lean years. So—the very first thing I want you to know about yourself is, that you and I and everyone on the surface of earth do have a special and unique talent to give to others. In fact, this special talent is so unique that *only* you can do it better than anyone else in the whole world. Just think of it! Furthermore; there is a unique need for your special talent—and, (here is the punch-line), ***when this need is 'matched' with the creative expression of your special and unique talent, that is when you ignite the spark in the creative mind of the universe, or the Higher Power, or the Source with or (whatever you want to call it) to conspire to work on your behalf.*** And, thus, help you access Its infinite, unbounded creativity and abundance. Expressing your special and unique talent to fulfill your own needs, could very well create an unlimited wealth and abundance in your own life. This is exactly what has happened in my own life. What I've discovered is that every adversity, every set-back, every heart-breaks in my own life, no matter how unjustified, no matter how unfair or how much uncalled for maybe, is in reality a blessing for me when I keep a positive attitude toward it. That is all.

The **second** thing that I want you to know about yourself is (and this is very important) that you have a definite major goal or purpose in life—and when you sort of *blend* your own special and unique talent with service to mankind or humanity—that is when you begin to think yourself as a soul and as a one with God—not just in some theory or an abstract principle but, a living, breathing, thinking, and living reality. What that means in plain language is that you have a m*ission in your own life for which only you were chosen to fulfill it.* **Think about this for a moment, Try to absorb the full significance of it.** If you get this second thing I want you to know about yourself, then, the most significant thing that can ever happen to a Soul, in a human body has already happened to you.

Your mission, should you choose to accept it, mainly deals with some service to humanity—to serve mankind for the highest good of all. Here's a direct quote from MSIA founder John-Roger that has personally helped me find out what my definite major goal, or purpose or mission (if you will) in life is—and how I can *blend* it to 'match' my special and unique talent to serve humanity or mankind. Then, suddenly, coincidences began to happen, that eventually led me to train myself as a Seminar Leader to host the MSIA Soul Awareness Seminars in my local community. Please understand that John-Roger's direct quote consists of three things that I endeavor to keep in my mind and they are my daily three guideline.

THREE GUIDE-LINES!

1. **Don't hurt yourself and don't hurt others.**
2. **Take care of yourself so you can help take care of others.**
3. **Use everything for your upliftment, growth and learning.**

Now—here's the bottom-line! *You'll have to find your own aim, goal, and purpose in life and then, fulfill it.* So—the big question is "how do you do that?"

Well, the eternal laws of nature, that teaches birds to fly, fish to swim, flowers to blossom, an acorn to change into a giant oak tree, and caterpillar into a beautiful butterfly—that's who? Once you learn the art of meditation as observation— and **Connect Heart with Head,** by opening the 'third-eye' and activating the Pineal gland of brain, you make the *Soul Connection in converging your spirit back into alignment the whole power of the universe is at your disposal to make it a reality in any way and every way possible in your life.*For me, I just imagine that there is a 'door' in the center of my chest which opens up and the bright, beautiful, divine LIGHT enters through the open door and my HEART opens up and this bright, beautiful, divine LIGHT enters the HEART travel through my back spine and meets the Pineal gland of brain ('third-eye') in the back of my head and *directs* the LIGHT to my forehead, behind the eyebrows and out into the universe and the internal becomes the external and begins to see the inner worlds of God through the Inner eye. One easy way I know that my 'third-eye' is open and my Spirit is back into alignment is that I feel the sensation of the Light traveling through my heart to the Pineal gland of my brain. I sense a faint pressure in my head and feel a 'tingle' in my mind. I notice with profound interest, the positive things are beginning to happen in my own life. My heart-energy begins to heal all my ailments. My spiritual goals are coming true. My worldly needs are met as if a miracle. I spend more time in spiritual pursuits—instead of reacting to world.

Finally, the key to remember is this: *I found my own special and unique talent in giving lectures and seminars to teach how to quickly open the 'third-eye' and activate the Pineal gland of the brain to assist me in converging Spirit back into alignment.* What that means in plain language is that I'm in *alignment* with the Left-Side and the Right-Side of my Spirit. Seeing the tiny 'dot' in red color or in black color or in blue or purple color in the back of my head, or seeing the total darkness in my forehead just behind the eyebrows, simply is an indication of the clear sign that I've been able to move the Left-Side and the Right-Side of the Spirit into the point of convergence where my Soul dwells in the middle of the both sides of the Spirit. Knowing that the Spirit is both—the Left-Sided and the Right-Sided Spirit (like negative and the positive poles of a battery), I remember that both sides are necessary to maintain balance of Spirit. The sad thing is that the division between the two sides of spirit is so delicate, it can take years of experience to learn to recognize the subtle energies emanating from the two sides. And so, many people deafen themselves to Spirit and begin to spin around the wheel of 84 and keep living here, and keep living here, and keep living here. And we say, I want to get-off the wheel of 84 because it's hard to live on this planet. The funny thing is that the Spirit does not care if you keep living here is fair or not fair. Spirit is ruthless. Spirit does not care how, where, or when It touches you. And, it does not care whether you want to stop the wheel of 84 now, last week, or in month, or never. Spirit moves on Its own and on Its own time. Any your job is to be ready to receive of the Spirit at any time and at all time. The convergence will shift!

CHAPTER 17

Take the Thirty-Day Mind-Theory Challenge

My spiritual teacher taught me that my own mind is my enemy because it will go against me in my Spirit. And it seems to win because although my Spirit, the Soul are a divine part of God—nevertheless; mind is a devil's advocate who will attempt to destroy any chances of ever converging my spirit back into alignment.

Mind is the thing inside of us that stops us from knowing what is going on. We don't belong here spiritually. That is why we have such a hard time making ourselves do according to our intention, because our intention only functions in the Spirit. When we attempt to take full and complete possession of our minds, that is when, *we come into alignment once again.* Do not let your thought and emotions (mind is both) move you; let your heart move you. It will; move you with its wisdom and knowledge. *Keep*

ever watchful. For the mind to trap you, it has to find a pattern of negativity in which you are involved, run it out in a time pattern, and lay a trap for you to fall into. In this last chapter, I will give information I have gained through my own thirty-five years experiencing controlling my own mind by taking the Mind-Theory Challenge. I share it here not as something to memorize and learn only mentally but as background information that you can have to avoid and bypass the pattern of negativity and lay the traps to fall into. Once you take the mind-theory challenge, the information I share with you will move out of 'theoretical-area' and become experiential. I will lead you step-by-step right now!

As with any muscle, the mind needs exercising to grow and stay in your own control. This thirty-day mind theory challenge will work for you—if you work it. It is a mental exercise that will teach you how to observe the mind-activity 24/7. I've personally experienced everything I'm teaching you here. It is a very practical way to control your own mind without the use of any self-suggestions or affirmations.

With Practice and persistence, you'll soon open-up a sort of a passageway to converge your Spirit back into alignment again—just by ***observing!*** Spiritual masters of all ages who have spent a life-time in spiritual pursuits—instead of reacting to te material world call ***observation*** the key to letting go. What I have found is that when I start to observe the 'mind-activity (self-talk or the internal dialogues of the mind), I notice with profound interest that the moment I observe the mind, suddenly all thinking of the mind begin to subside and eventually leave the mind. It is as the mind is without any thoughts. In the East, it's called the 'no—mind'. My mind is totally under my own control and would not dare start its incessant, compulsive thinking. It's a feeling that I never get tired of. I stop reacting emotionally, and I don not get thrown-off balance. My spiritual teacher used to say that only human beings are capable of observing the presence of God in all things, including myself. Human beings are sacred and superior to all of other God's creation for that very reason—power to control the mind **just by observing it's thoughts**. If only we as human beings could understand that simple fact, I believe that we will not have such a hard time making ourselves do what we want to do according to our intention, because our intention only functions in the Spirit!

Here's how it works. For the next thirty-days, simply refused to let any negative thoughts linger in your own mind. The moment that you realize that you are dwelling on any negative thoughts—just start observing them. You'll notice that all those negative thoughts will

begin to subside—and—eventually leave your own mind. Now—here is the challenge for you: If you dwell on any negative thoughts of the mind for more than five minutes at a time, you have failed the challenge and need to start all over again, next week. As you start the thirty-day mind-theory challenge, just keep in mind that there is no such thing as a free lunch (so to speak). You must pay the price in time and persistence if want to conquer your own mind. It may surprise you, nevertheless; it is absolutely true that I was ready, able, willing to sacrifice anything and everything, but not my God—given right and the privilege to take full and complete possession of my own mind by taking the thirty-day mind-theory challenge—and I meant it—*literally!* For the next thirty-days, take this challenge. Simply refused to let any negative thought and emotion to linger in your own mind. Just observe the mind-chatter, the self—talk of the mind, the internal dialogues of the mind until they begin to subside and eventually leave the mind. Such is the power of observation. To learn a skill, you must be able and willing to work hard at it. Know this, 80 to 90 percent of all mind activity is usually negative, useless, repetitive, and involuntarily. Just think of it! I mean, how do you suppose that kind of negative thinking impact our daily life? If you take the challenge for 30-days and have a mind without any thoughts, *you'll become aware of your thoughts* <u>without</u> *being any part of mind's thinking!*

Author's Notes

This book is a reflection of my own spiritual understanding of the subject under discussion. It isn't intended to speak for any other modern-day religion or a spiritual path. Please understand, that I am in no way more gifted, more special or more spiritual than you. For thirty-five years I have been on my own personal spiritual path and have worked under several Spiritual masters. I have occasionally used terms that mean different things to different people, depending upon either the religious upbringing, or the personal path they have chosen. Some people might find my own writing style a little stilted for their own taste. I write in the way I'm guided from within—and nothing in this book have come from my own intellect or intelligence —I assure you. After thirty-five years of search for a true spiritual path that coincide with my own intuitively knowing of myself as a Soul—and as a one with God—I've personally found a spiritual path—known as the *Movement of Spiritual Inner Awareness*—called MSIA for short. What is MSIA? You may ask:

My answer: MSIA— is a non-denominational, ecumenical church, incorporated in the State of California as non-profit organization, based in Los Angeles, CA.MSIA serves a few thousands students in six continents. ***The purpose is to teach Soul Transcendence, which is becoming aware of yourself as a Soul—and as a one with God—not in theory, but a living daily reality in life.*** This movement was begun by a man named ***John-Roger***—who held the 'inner-keys' to the Mystical Traveler Consciousness.

This **mantle** was passed on to **John Morton, the spiritual director of MSIA. We are finding that people coming into MSIA**, around the world, are very spiritual—and yet **not—religious!** *For many years, home seminars led by John- Roger—the founder of MSIA were* **the backbone of MSIA.** Over the years, thousands have been introduced to the Traveler's teachings. In the early days of MSIA, when the number of people involved in the Movement was fairly small, John-Roger presented the Traveler teachings at fireside seminars in the intimate setting of people's homes.

Today, the essence of loving and uplifting he brought forward can still be experienced in home seminars across the planet. MSIA has almost 1,400 active seminar leaders in twenty-nine different countries, including Russia, Greece, Israel, and Japan. MSIA—gratefully acknowledges the worldwide family of devoted seminar leaders. They provide a consistent, reliable, and safe harbor for those who are looking for the Traveler's teachings. As a seminar leader, I am an important part of the Traveler's work in my local community. We offer monthly events for folks who are very spiritual—but not necessarily religious. Our seminars provide the opportunity for people to come together into greater communion with the Traveler and Spirit. Seminars, by their very design, support the awakening of people, in their own way and in their own timing, to the greatest reality of who they are. So—people receive the benefit simply by gathering with others holding an intention to learn and grow spiritually! My job, as MSIA Soul Awareness Seminar Leader is to hold the Light, which encourages the group to move forward a loving consciousness—it's that simple!

AFTERWORD

An Excerpt from the book:
Spiritual Warrior
By John-Roger

"Here is the paradox:
Spirit has always been there.
And for the most part,
We have always been there.
If we have been there,
And it has been there, why are we not
knowing that we are both there?"

Models of the Spiritual Warrior

(An Invitation)

"It has been said that there are no heroes these days. The same might be said of Spiritual Warriors; there are none today. J-R has intuitively instructed me to ask the MSIA community to include a list of people, real or fictional who represent the characteristics of the Spiritual Warrior to you. Name the person, and describe the Spiritual Warrior characteristics they demonstrate to you.

Call Mushtaq (Jeff) Jaaafri (909) 344-0167 or

Send email: mushtaqjaafri@gmail.com

Much Light and Love.

Thank You!

My Daily 24/7 Challenge

My Spiritual teacher once challenged me to validate and prove to the world that: *"The mantle of the Spiritual Warrior is attainable by everyone.* But, I must admit to you that it requires a different way of proceeding through life, one which will be challenging." My Spiritual teacher also said that if I do accept and take the daily 24/7 challenge, and are willing to practice the art of the Spiritual Warrior life-style then, I will find the rewards are tremendous. It is the satisfaction that comes to all who *conquer self and force life to pay whatever is asked."* But, let me be perfectly honest with you and tell you that the task of developing and incorporating the characteristics of living the **Spiritual Warrior** life-style is formidable. But, I will say this if you are willing to practice—your habits will trap you—to God and not the mind. He said: **"we need constantly to shape up the old habits and make room for new habits.** More importantly, we need to practice **being in Spirit."** He continued: "Spiritual Warrior counters negative habits and destructive relationships by changing patterns and **living in conscious alignment with the Soul.** In this book, I attempt to lay out not only the problems but also give the practical Solutions. (Fifteen Spiritual Exercises in Chapter Eight, for instance). For me, living in conscious alignment with my Soul, was the hardest task to master. It literally took my thirty-five years of searching until I did conquer the self and force life pay-off in terms of my own choosing. One easy way for me to align with me Soul is that when a thought comes in my mind, I don't fight or judge but observe!

Excerpt from the book: *Spiritual Warrior* – by John-Roger, D.S.S

The Heart: An Exercise in Loving Yourself

"Try Reading the following into a CD recorder. Then play it back and **observe,** hearing not yourself, but the Spirit speaking to you. *It is the Spirit that speaks the words to your heart. Listen to that heart, and fill it up with Divinity. Breath it, feel the heart expanding, and feel the energy in your heart. Take a few moment to touch this heart area. You can put both your hands over it and just know that Divinity and the loving exist. Just know that, and feel it.* If you get goose bumps, or you sharply inhale, or you experience energy moving, that is an indication that you are starting to move into it. Stay present with it: *don't move your mind to something else. Only do this. Stay with this.* Placing your hands over the heart keep you kinesthetically ties to it. *Tell yourself, "This is love...."* Now if some place in your body does not feel well, just have that love extend over and touch it. If you start to move away from it, bring it back. Touch it again and feel it. *Say, This is Divinity. This is love. This is where it is inside of me.* From my heart and my heart center I give love to all my body." If you feel a funny feeling sensation in your stomach, reach down and touch it. *Say, "This love arcs to that or goes through*

that." If you are not having success, think of someone you really love your spouse, your child, your life, God. Take that feeling and make it come awake in your heart, because it is your Divinity. It is yours. When that hits, flood your body with it and you will find yourself being a commutator of Divine energy and it will be flooding down all around you. Love is the healer. Joy is the expression."

Excerpt from the book: *Spiritual Warrior* **– by John-Roger, D.S.S**

Tool of the Spiritual Warrior: Spiritual Exercises

In the MSIA teaching lingo, the Spiritual exercises are often referred to as (s.e's) and designed to help us break through the illusions of the lower levels and move into an increased awareness of the Soul." What I have found is that s.e's is an active technique of *bypassing* the mind and emotions by providing me a focus of my awareness as I move along my intention. *Fifteen Spiritual Exercises in chapter eight of this book has literally assisted me in converging my spirit back into alignment and to connect with the energy that flows from God. The key to remember is that the only wrong way to do s.e.'s is not to do them.* So—there are no rules, rituals, or postures that are necessary to begin my practice. **S.e.s are an an action of the heart, in which the approach is one developed and a clear intention to know Spirit and God in a greater way.** Having said this that, for those who would like to have some form of methodology so they can begin their *Fifteen-Day Spiritual* s.e.'s as outlined in the chapter eight of this book, here is a step-by-step procure as a suggestion for doing fifteen minutes of s.e.'s. 1. Find a quiet place with low lighting and comfortable chair to sit in.2, Sit straight, and close your eyes. If you find wandering and you lose the focus of reading the designated passage, you can focus the mind *observing.* In the East, this is called the **Meditation as Observation**. My Spiritual teacher often said that: *"this kind ofs.e.'s can make you to be as deep, as ecstatic, as God-intoxicated as you want to be.* Meditation as Observation is the easiest process in the world.

NOTES

NOTES

Printed in the United States
By Bookmasters